PUZZLES &
PERPLEXITIES

PUZZLES &
PERPLEXITIES

Collected Essays

STEVEN M. CAHN

ROWMAN & LITTLEFIELD PUBLISHERS, INC.
Lanham • Boulder • New York • Oxford

ROWMAN & LITTLEFIELD PUBLISHERS, INC.

Published in the United States of America
by Rowman & Littlefield Publishers, Inc.
A Member of the Rowman & Littlefield Publishing Group
4720 Boston Way, Lanham, Maryland 20706
www.rowmanlittlefield.com

PO Box 317
Oxford
OX2 9RU, UK

British Library Cataloguing in Publication Information Available

Library of Congress Cataloging-in-Publication Data

Cahn, Steven M.
   Puzzles and perplexities : collected essays / Steven M. Cahn.
     p. cm
   Includes bibliographical references.
   ISBN 0-7425-1422-6 (alk. paper) — ISBN 0-7425-1423-4
(pbk. : alk. paper)
   1. Philosophy. 2. Education—Philosophy. I. Title.
  BD41.C26 2002
  191—dc21

2002009075

Printed in the United States of America

♾™ The paper used in this publication meets the minimum requirements of
American National Standard for Information Sciences—Permanence of Paper for
Printed Library Materials, ANSI/NISO Z39.48-1992.

To the memory of my parents,

JUDAH CAHN,
who introduced me to both biblical exegesis and
philosophical inquiry, and

EVELYN BAUM CAHN,
a teacher, beloved by her high school students
and adored by her two sons.

CONTENTS

Part IV. Education

PREFACE

The materials collected here have appeared over a period of nearly forty years, and explore primarily philosophical and educational issues. The reprinted versions are mostly unchanged but for matters of style.

My views were shaped significantly by my undergraduate studies with Ernest Nagel, my graduate studies with Richard Taylor, the influences of Charles Frankel and Sidney Hook, and numerous conversations with my colleagues John O'Connor, James Rachels, George Sher, and David Rosenthal. I have also learned much from my longtime friends Ronald J. Bettauer, Leon Bramson, George F. Farr, Jr., and the late Geoffrey Marshall.

I also wish to express my appreciation to the students and advisees over the years who have responded warmly to my guidance and, in turn, inspired my thinking. Space does not permit my mentioning more than a few of the many I remember, but I want here to acknowledge Martha (Theo) DeWitt, Maureen Eckert, Robert Gurland, Tziporah Kasachkoff, Peter Markie, David Shatz, Robert Talisse, and Andrea Tschemplik.

Finally, I am most grateful to my editor, Eve DeVaro, for her enthusiastic assistance; to Jon Sisk, publisher of Rowman & Littlefield, for his longtime support; to my brother, Victor L. Cahn, for so many years of wise counsel, stylistic and otherwise; and to my wife, Marilyn, for more than I can express in words.

I

FREE WILL

1

FREE WILL OR DETERMINISM?

In 1924 the American people were horrified by a senseless crime of extraordinary brutality. The defendants were eighteen-year-old Nathan Leopold and seventeen-year-old Richard Loeb, the sons of Chicago millionaires, and brilliant students who had led seemingly idyllic lives. Leopold was the youngest graduate in the history of the University of Chicago, and Loeb the youngest graduate in the history of the University of Michigan. Suddenly they were accused of the kidnapping and vicious murder of fourteen-year-old Bobby Franks, a cousin of Loeb's. Before the trial even began, Leopold and Loeb both confessed, and from across the country came an outcry for their execution.

The lawyer who agreed to defend them was Clarence Darrow, the outstanding defense attorney of his time. Since Leopold and Loeb had already admitted their crime, Darrow's only chance was to explain their behavior in such a way that his clients could escape the death penalty. He was forced to argue that Leopold and Loeb were not morally responsible for what they had done, that they were not to be blamed for their actions. But how could he possibly maintain that position?

Darrow's defense was a landmark in the history of criminal law. He argued that the actions of his clients were a direct and necessary result of hereditary and environmental forces beyond their control.[1] Leopold suffered from a glandular disease that left him depressed and moody. Originally shy with girls, he had been sent to an all-girls school as a cure, but had sustained deep psychic scars from which he never recovered. In addition, his parents instilled in him the belief that his wealth absolved him of any responsibility toward others. Pathologically inferior because of his diminutive size, and pathologically superior because of his wealth, he became an acute schizophrenic.

Loeb suffered from a nervous disorder that caused fainting spells. During his unhappy childhood, he had often thought of committing suicide. He was under the control of a domineering governess and was forced to lie and cheat to deceive her. His wealth led him to believe that he was superior to all those around him, and he developed a fascination for crime, an activity in which he could demonstrate his superiority. By the time he reached college he was severely psychotic.

In his final plea, Darrow recounted these facts. His central theme was that Leopold and Loeb were in the grip of powers beyond their control, that they themselves were victims.

> I do not know what it was that made these boys do this mad act, but I do know there is a reason for it. I know they did not beget themselves. I know that any one of an infinite number of causes reaching back to the beginning might be working out in these boys' minds, whom you are asked to hang in malice and in hatred and in injustice, because someone in the past has sinned against them. . . . What had this boy to do with it? He was not his own father; he was not his own mother; he was not his own grandparents. All of this was handed to him. He did not surround himself with governesses and wealth. He did not make himself. And yet he is to be compelled to pay.[2]

Darrow's plea was successful, for Leopold and Loeb escaped execution and were sentenced to life imprisonment. Although they had committed crimes and were legally responsible for their actions, the judge believed they were not morally responsible, for they had not acted freely.

If the line of argument that Darrow utilized in the Leopold–Loeb case is sound, then not only were Leopold and Loeb not to blame for what they had done, but no person is ever to blame for any actions. As Darrow himself put it, "We are all helpless."[3] But is Darrow's argument sound? Does the conclusion follow from the premises, and are the premises true?

We can formalize his argument as follows:

Premise 1: No action is free if it must occur.
Premise 2: In the case of every event that occurs, antecedent conditions, known or unknown, ensure the event's occurrence.
Conclusion: Therefore, no action is free.

Premise (1) assumes that an action is free only if it is within the agent's power to perform it and within the agent's power not to perform it. In other words, whether a free action will occur is up to the agent. If circumstances require the agent to perform a certain action or require the agent not to perform that action, then the action is not free.

Premise (2) is the thesis known as "determinism." Put graphically, it is the claim that if at any time a being knew the position of every particle in the universe and all the forces acting on each particle, then that being could predict with certainty every future event. Determinism does not presume such a being exists; the being is only imagined in order to illustrate what the world would be like if determinism were true.

Darrow's conclusion, which is supposed to follow from premises (1) and (2), is that no person has free will. Note that to have free will does not imply being free with regard to all actions, for only the mythical Superman is free to leap tall buildings at a single bound. But so long as at least some of an agent's actions are free, the agent is said to have free will. What Darrow's argument purports to prove is that not a single human action that has ever been performed has been performed freely.

Does the conclusion of Darrow's argument follow from the premises? If premise (2) is true, then every event that occurs must occur, for its occurrence is ensured by antecedent conditions. Since every action is an event, it follows from premise (2) that every action that occurs must occur. But according to premise (1), no action is free if it must occur. Thus, if premises (1) and (2) are true, it follows that no action is free—the conclusion of Darrow's argument.

Even granting that Darrow's reasoning is unassailable, we need not accept the conclusion of his argument unless we grant the truth of his premises. Should we do so?

Hard determinism is the view that both premises of Darrow's argument are correct. In other words, a hard determinist believes that determinism is true and that, as a consequence, no person has free will.[4] Determinists note that whenever an event occurs, we all assume that a causal explanation can account for the occurrence of the event. Suppose, for example, you feel a pain in your arm and are prompted to visit a physician. After examining you, the doctor announces that the pain had no cause, either physical or psychological. In other words, you were supposed to be suffering from an uncaused pain. On hearing this diagnosis, you would surely switch doctors. After all, no one may be able to discover the cause of your pain, but surely something is causing it. If nothing were causing it, you wouldn't be in pain. This same line of reasoning applies whether the event to be explained is a loud noise, a change in the weather, or an individual's action. If the event were uncaused, it wouldn't have occurred.

However, we may agree that the principle of determinism holds in the vast majority of cases, yet doubt is applicability in the realm of human action. While causal explanations may be found for rocks falling and birds flying, people are far more complex than rocks or birds.

The determinist responds to this objection by asking us to consider any specific action: for instance, your decision to read this book. You may suppose your decision was uncaused, but did you not wish to acquire information about philosophy? The determinist argues that your desire for such information, together with your belief that the information is found in this book, caused you to read. Just as physical forces cause rocks and birds to do things, so human actions are caused by desires and beliefs.

If you doubt this claim, the determinist can call attention to our success in predicting people's behavior. For example, a store owner who reduces prices can depend on increasing visits by shoppers; an athlete who wins a major championship can rely on greater attention from the press. Furthermore, when we read novels or see plays, we expect to understand why the characters act as they do, and an author who fails to provide such explanations is charged with poor writing. The similarity of people's reactions to the human condition also accounts for the popularity of the incisive psychological insights of a writer such as La Rochefoucauld, the French aphorist. We read one of his maxims, for instance, "When our integrity declines, our taste does also,"[5] and nod our heads with approval, but are we not agreeing to a plausible generalization about the workings of the human psyche?

Granted, people's behavior cannot be predicted with certainty, but the hard determinist reminds us that each individual is influenced by a unique combination of hereditary and environmental factors. Just as each rock is slightly different from every other rock, and each bird is somewhat different from every other bird, so human beings differ from each other. But just as rocks and birds are part of an unbroken chain of causes and effects, so human beings, too, are part of that chain. Just as a rock falls because it breaks off from a cliff, so people act because of their desires and beliefs. And just as a rock has no control over the wind that causes it to break off, so people have no control over the desires and beliefs that cause them to act. In short, we are said to have no more control over our desires and beliefs than Leopold and Loeb had over theirs. If you can control your desire for food and your friend cannot, the explanation is that your will is of a sort that can control your desire and your friend's will is of a sort that cannot. That your will is of one sort and your friend's will of another is not within the control of either of you. As one hard determinist has written, "If we can overcome the effects of early environment, the ability to do so is itself a product of the early environment. We did not give ourselves this ability; and if we lack it we cannot be blamed for not having it."[6]

At this point in the argument an antideterminist is apt to call attention to recent developments in physics that have been interpreted by some thinkers as a refutation of determinism. They claim that work in quantum mechanics demonstrates that certain subatomic events are uncaused and inherently unpredictable. Yet some physicists and philosophers of science argue that determinism has not been refuted, since the experimental results can be understood in causal terms.[7] The outcome of this dispute, however, seems irrelevant to the issue of human freedom, since the events we are discussing are not subatomic, and indeterminism on that level is compatible with the universal causation of events on the much larger level of human action.

Here, then, is a summary of hard determinism: According to this view, determinism is true and no person has free will. Every event that occurs is caused to occur, for otherwise why would it occur? Your present actions are events caused by your previous desires and beliefs, which themselves are accounted for by hereditary and environmental factors. These are part of a causal chain extending back far before your birth, and each link of the chain determines the succeeding link. Since you obviously have no control over events that occurred before your birth, and since these earlier events determined the later ones, it follows that you have no control over your present actions. In short, you do not have free will.

The hard determinist's argument may appear plausible, yet few of us are inclined to accept its shocking conclusion. We opt, therefore, to deny one of its two premises. *Soft determinism* is the view that the conclusion is false because premise (1) is false. In other words, a soft determinist believes both that determinism is true and that human beings have free will. The implication of the position is that an action may be free even if it is part of a causal chain extending back to events outside the agent's control. While this view may at first appear implausible, it has been defended throughout the centuries by many eminent philosophers, including Hume and Mill.

An approach employed explicitly or implicitly by many soft determinists has come to be known as "the paradigm-case argument." Consider it first in another setting, where its use is a classic of philosophical argumentation.

In studying physics, we learn that ordinary objects like tables and chairs are composed of sparsely scattered, minute particles. This fact may lead us to suppose that such objects are not solid. As Sir Arthur Eddington, the noted physicist, put it, a "plank has no solidity of substance. To step on it is like stepping on a swarm of flies."[8]

Eddington's view that a plank is not solid was forcefully attacked by the British philosopher L. Susan Stebbing. She pointed out that the word "solid" derives its meaning from examples such as planks.

> For "solid" just is the word we use to describe a certain respect in which a plank of wood resembles a block of marble, a piece of paper, and a cricket ball, and in which each of these differs from a sponge, from the interior of a soap-bubble, and from the holes in a net. . . . The point is that the common usage of language enables us to attribute a meaning to the phrase "a solid plank"; but there is no common usage of language that provides a meaning for the word "solid" that would make sense to say that the plank on which I stand is not solid.[9]

In other words, a plank is a paradigm case of solidity. Anyone who claims that a plank is not solid does not know how the word "solid" is used in the English language. Note that Stebbing is not criticizing Eddington's scientific views but only the manner in which he interpreted them.

The paradigm-case argument is useful to soft determinists, for in the face of the hard determinist's claim that no human action is free, soft determinists respond by pointing to a paradigm case of a free action, for instance, a person walking down the street. They stipulate that the individual is not under the influence of drugs, is not attached to ropes, is not sleepwalking, and so on; in other words, they refer to a normal, everyday instance of a person walking down the street. Soft determinists claim that the behavior described is a paradigm case of a free action, clearly distinguishable from instances in which a person is, in fact, under the influence of drugs, attached to ropes, or sleepwalking. These latter cases are not examples of free actions, or are at best problematic examples, while the case the soft determinists cite is clear and seemingly indisputable. Indeed, according to soft determinists, anyone who claims the act of walking down the street is not free does not know how the word "free" is used in English. Thus people certainly have free will, for we can cite obvious cases in which they act freely.

How do soft determinists define a "free action"? According to them, actions are free if the persons who perform them wish to do so and could, if they wished, not perform them. If your arm is forcibly raised, you did not act freely, for you did not wish to raise your arm. If you were locked in a room, you would also not be free, even if you wished to be there, for if you wished to leave, you couldn't.

Soft determinists emphasize that once we define "freedom" correctly, any apparent incompatibility between freedom and determinism will disappear. Consider come particular action I perform that is free in the sense explicated by soft determinists. Granting that the action is one link in a causal chain extending far back beyond my birth, nevertheless, I am free with regard to that action, for I wish to perform it, and if I did not wish to, I would not do so. This description of the situation is consistent with supposing that my wish is a result of hereditary and environmental factors over which I have no control. The presence of such factors is, according to the soft determinists, irrelevant to the question of whether my action is free. I may be walking down a particular street because of my desire to buy a coat and my belief that I am heading toward a clothing store, and this desire and belief may themselves be caused by any number of other factors. But since I desire to walk down the street and could walk down some other street if I so desired, it follows that I am freely walking down the street. By this line of reasoning soft determinists affirm both free will and determinism, finding no incompatibility between them.

Soft determinism is an inviting doctrine, for it allows us to maintain a belief in free will without having to relinquish the belief that every event has a cause. Soft determinism, however, is open to objections that have led some philosophers to abandon the position.

The fundamental problem for soft determinists is that their definition of "freedom" does not seem in accordance with the ordinary way in which we use the term. Note that soft determinists and hard determinists offer two different definitions of "freedom." According to the hard determinist, an action is free if it is within my power to perform it and also within my power not to perform it. According to the soft determinist, an action is free if it is such that if I wish to perform it I may, and if I wish not to perform it I also may. To highlight the difference between these definitions, consider the case of a man who has been hypnotized and rolls up the leg of his pants as if to cross a stream. Is his action free? According to the hard determinist, the man's action is not free, for it is not within his power to refrain from rolling up the leg of his pants. According to the soft determinist's definition of "freedom," the action would be considered free, for the agent desires to perform it, and if he didn't desire to, he wouldn't. But a man under hypnosis is not free. Therefore, the soft determinist's definition of "freedom" seems unsatisfactory.

Perhaps this objection to soft determinism is unfair, since the desires of the hypnotized man are not his own but are controlled by the hypnotist. The force of the objection to soft determinism, however, is that the soft determinist overlooks whether a person's wishes or desires are themselves within that individual's control. The hard determinist emphasizes that my action is free only if it is up to me whether to perform it. But in order for an action to be up to me, I need to have control over my own wishes or desires. If I do not, my desires might be controlled by a hypnotist, a brainwasher, my family, hereditary factors, and so on, and thus I would not be free. Soft determinists do not appear to take such possibilities seriously, since, according to them, I would be free even if my desires were not within my control, so long as I was acting according to my desires and could act differently if my desires were different. But could my desires have been different? That is the crucial question. If my desires could not have been different, then I could not have acted in any way other than I did. And that is the description of a person who is not free.

By failing to consider the ways in which a person's desires can be controlled by external forces beyond the individual's control, soft determinists offer a definition of "freedom" that I find not in accord with our normal use of the term. They may, of course, define terms as they wish, but we are interested in the concept of freedom relevant to questions of moral responsibility. Any concept of freedom implying that hypnotized or brainwashed individuals are morally responsible for their actions is not the concept in question.

What of the soft determinist's claim that a person's walking down the street is a paradigm case of a free action? Although I agree that the paradigm-case argument can sometimes be used effectively, the soft determinist's appeal to it does not seem convincing. To see why, imagine that we traveled to a land in which the inhabitants believed that every woman born on February 29 was a witch, and that every witch had the power to cause droughts. If we refused to believe that any woman was a witch, the philosophically sophisticated inhabitants might try to convince us by appealing to the paradigm-case argument, claiming that anyone born on February 29 is a paradigm case of a witch.

What would we say in response? How does this appeal to a paradigm case differ from Susan Stebbing's appeal to a plank as a paradigm case of solidity? No one doubts that a plank can hold significant weight and is, in that sense, solid. But until women born on February 29 demonstrate supernatural powers and are in that sense witches, the linguistic claim alone has no force.

Are soft determinists appealing to an indisputable instance when they claim that a person's walking down the street is a paradigm case of a free action? Not at all, for as we saw in the trial of Leopold and Loeb, such apparently free actions may not turn out to be judged as free. By appealing to a disputable example as a paradigm case, soft determinists assume what they are supposed to be proving. They are supposed to demonstrate that actions such as walking down the street are examples of free actions. Merely asserting that such actions are free is to overlook the hard determinist's argument that such actions are not free. No questionable instance can be used as a paradigm case, and walking down the street is, as Darrow demonstrated, a questionable example of a free action. So soft determinism appears to have a serious weakness.

Remember that the hard determinist argues that since premises (1) and (2) of Darrow's argument are true, so is the conclusion. Soft determinists argue that premise (1) is false. If they are mistaken, then the only way to avoid hard determinism is to reject premise (2). That position is known as "libertarianism."

The *libertarian* agrees with the hard determinist that if an action must occur, it is not free. For the libertarian as well as for the hard determinist, I am free with regard to a particular action only if it is within my power to perform the action and within my power not to perform it. But do persons ever act freely? The hard determinist believes that people are never free, since in the case of every action antecedent conditions, known or unknown, ensure the action's occurrence. Libertarians refuse to accept this conclusion, but find it impossible to reject premise (1) of Darrow's argument. So their only recourse is to reject premise (2). As Sherlock Holmes noted, "When you have eliminated the impossible, whatever remains, however improbable, must be the truth."[10] The libertarian thus denies that every event has a cause.

But why is the libertarian so convinced that people sometimes act freely? Consider an ordinary human action, for instance, raising your hand at a meeting to attract the speaker's attention. If you are attending a lecture and the time comes for questions from the audience, you believe it is within your power to raise your hand and also within your power not to raise it. The choice is yours. Nothing forces you to ask a question, and nothing prevents you from asking one. What could be more obvious? If this description of the situation is accurate, then hard determinism is incorrect, for you are free with regard to the act of raising your hand.

The heart of the libertarian's position is that innumerable examples of this sort are conclusive evidence for free will. Indeed, we normally accept them as such. We assume on most occasions that we are free with regard to our actions, and, moreover, we assume that other persons are free with regard to theirs. If a friend agrees to meet us at six o'clock for dinner and arrives an hour late claiming to have lost track of time, we blame her for her tardiness, since we assume she had it within her power to act otherwise. All she had to do was glance at her watch, and assuming no special circumstances were involved, it was within her power to do so. She was simply negligent and deserves to be blamed, for she could have acted conscientiously. But to believe she could have acted in a way other than she did is to believe she was free.

How do hard determinists respond to such examples? They argue that such situations need to be examined in greater detail. In the case of our friend who arrives an hour late for dinner, we assume she is to blame for her actions, but the hard determinist points out that some motive impelled her to be late. Perhaps she was more interested in finishing her work at the office than in arriving on time for dinner. But why was she more interested in finishing her work than in arriving on time? Perhaps because her parents instilled in her the importance of work but not promptness. Hard determinists stress that whatever the explanation for her lateness, the motive causing it was stronger than the motive impelling her to arrive on time. She acted as she did because her strongest motive prevailed. Which motive was the strongest, however, was not within her control, and so she was not free.

The hard determinist's rely may seem persuasive. How can I deny that I am invariably caused to act by my strongest motive? But analysis reveals that the thesis is tautological, immune from refutation, and so devoid of empirical content. For no matter what example of a human action is presented, a defender of the thesis could argue that the person's action resulted from the strongest motive. If I take a swim, taking a swim must have been my strongest motive. If I decide to forgo the swim and read a book instead, then reading a book must have been my strongest motive. How do we know that my motive to read a book was stronger than my motive to take a swim? Because I read a book and did not take a swim. If this line of argument appears powerful, the illusion will last only so long as we do not ask how we are to identify a person's strongest motive. For the only possible answer appears to be that the strongest motive is the motive that prevails, the motive that causes the person to act. If the strongest motive is the motive causing the person to act, what force is there in the claim that the motive causing a person to act is causing the person to act? No insight into the complexities of human action is obtained by trumpeting such an empty redundancy.

Thus the hard determinist does not so easily succeed in overturning the examples of free actions offered by the libertarian. But both hard and soft determinists have another argument to offer against the libertarian's position. If the libertarian is correct that free actions are uncaused, why do they occur? Are they inexplicable occurrences? If so, to act freely would be to act in a random, chaotic, unintelligible fashion. Yet it is unreasonable to hold people morally blameworthy for inexplicable actions. If you are driving a car and, to your surprise, find yourself turning the wheel to the right, we can hardly blame you if an accident occurs, for what happened was beyond your control.

So determinists argue that libertarians are caught in a dilemma. If we are caused to do whatever we do, libertarians assert we are not morally responsible for our actions. Yet if our actions are uncaused and inexplicable, libertarians again must deny our moral responsibility. How then can libertarians claim we ever act responsibly?

To understand the libertarian response, consider the simple act of a man picking up a telephone receiver. Suppose we want to understand what he is doing and are told he is calling his stockbroker. The man has decided to buy some stock and wishes his broker to place the appropriate order. With this explanation, we now know why this man has picked up the telephone. Although we may be interested in learning more about the man or his choice of stocks, we have a complete explanation of his action, which turns out not to be random, chaotic, or unintelligible. We may not know what, if anything, is causing the man to act, but we do know the reason for the man's action. The libertarian thus replies to the determinist's dilemma by arguing that an action can be uncaused yet understandable, explicable in terms of the agent's intentions or purposes.

Now contrast the libertarian's description of a particular action with a determinist's. Let the action be you moving your arm to adjust your television set. A determinist claims you were caused to move your arm by your desire to adjust the set and your belief that you could make this adjustment by turning the dials. A libertarian claims you moved your arm in order to adjust the set.

Note that the libertarian explains human actions fundamentally differently from the way in which we explain the movements of rocks or rivers. If we speak of a rock's purpose in falling off a cliff or a river's purpose in flowing south, we do so only metaphorically, for we believe that rocks and rivers have no purposes of their own but are caused to do what they do. Strictly speaking, a rock does not fall in order to hit the ground, and a river does not flow in order to reach the south. But libertarians are speaking not metaphorically but literally when they say that people act in order to achieve their purposes. After all, not even the most complex machine can act as a person does. A machine can break down and fail to operate, but only a human being can protest and stop work on purpose.

Is the libertarian's view correct? I doubt anyone is justified in answering that question with certainty, but if the libertarian is right, human beings are often morally responsible for their actions. They deserve praise when acting admirably and blame when acting reprehensibly. Darrow may have been correct in arguing that Leopold and Loeb were not free agents, but if the libertarian is right, the burden of proof lay with Darrow, for he had to demonstrate that these boys were in that respect unlike the rest of us.

But what if the libertarian is not correct? What if all human actions are caused by antecedent conditions, known or unknown, that ensure their occurrence? Then moral responsibility would vanish, but even so people could be held legally responsible for their actions. Just as we need to be safeguarded against mad dogs, so we need protection from dangerous people. Thus, even if no person were morally responsible, we would still have a legal system, courts, criminals, and prisons. Remember that Darrow's eloquence did not free his clients; indeed, he did not ask that they be freed. Although he did not blame them for their actions, he did not want those actions repeated. To Darrow, Leopold and Loeb were sick men who needed the same care as sick persons with a contagious disease. After all, in a world without freedom, events need not be viewed as agreeable; they should, however, be understood as necessary.

NOTES

1. The following information is found in Irving Stone's *Clarence Darrow for the Defense* (Garden City, N.Y.: Doubleday, Doran, 1941), pp. 384–391.

2. *Attorney for the Damned*, ed. Arthur Weinberg (New York: Simon and Schuster, 1957), pp. 37, 65.

3. *Ibid.*, p. 37.

4. The expressions "hard determinism" and "soft determinism" were coined by William James in his essay "The Dilemma of Determinism," reprinted in *Essays on Faith and Morals* (Cleveland: World, 1962).

5. *The Maxims of La Rochefoucauld*, trans. Louis Kronenberger (New York: Random House, 1959), #379.

6. John Hospers, "What Means This Freedom," in *Determinism and Freedom in the Age of Modern Science*, ed. Sidney Hook (New York: Collier, 1961), p. 138.

7. For a detailed discussion of the philosophical implications of quantum mechanics, see Ernest Nagel's *The Structure of Science* (New York: Harcourt Brace Jovanovich, 1961), ch. 10.

8. A. S. Eddington, *The Nature of the Physical World* (New York: Macmillan, 1928), p. 342.

9. L. Susan Stebbing, *Philosophy and the Physicists* (New York: Dover, 1958), pp. 51–52.

10. Sir Arthur Conan Doyle, "The Sign of Four," in *The Complete Sherlock Holmes* (Garden City, N.Y.: Doubleday, n.d.), p. 111.

2

RANDOM CHOICES

The libertarian claim that the doctrine of free will can be true only if determinism is false has often been attacked on the grounds that "what is random is no more free than what is caused."[1] As A. J. Ayer argues:

> Either it is an accident that I choose to act as I do or it is not. If it is an accident, then it is merely a matter of chance that I did not choose otherwise; and if it is merely a matter of chance that I did not choose otherwise, it is surely irrational to hold me morally responsible for choosing as I did. But if it is not an accident that I choose to do one thing rather than another, then presumably there is some causal explanation of my choice; and in that case we are led back to determinism.[2]

I want to call attention to a common phenomenon that has not often been the subject of philosophical concern, but that on examination suggests that a random act, although seemingly uncaused, need be neither accidental nor irresponsible.

We are frequently called on to make a conscious choice from among alternatives that are exactly equal in their degree of attractiveness or unattractiveness: "Pick a card." "Choose a number from 1 to 10." "Park your car in any of the available spaces." "Have a cupcake." Normally none of us has any difficulty making such a random choice. But how do we manage to perform this seemingly simple task? How do we decide which card to pick or which number to choose?

At a party you are offered a bowl of apples. You reach out, choose one, take it in your hand, and eat it. The following conversation ensues:

Host: "Why did you choose that one?"
Guest: "I just picked one, any one. You said, 'Take one.' So I did."

15

Host: "But why did you take that one? You could have taken any of the others. Don't they look as good? What led you to make that particular choice?"
Guest: "I don't know. I just chose."

At the store you buy one box of corn flakes rather than another, although other boxes appear equally wholesome. In the park you sit on one bench rather than another, although others would serve equally well. While writing a philosophical paper, you choose "Jones" as an example of a proper name, although "Smith" would be equally appropriate. None of these decisions causes you any anguish; they are all made with ease.

Can such random choices be explained? Of course, we can explain a person's deciding to spend money on corn flakes rather than prunes—although some philosophers would say such an explanation must be ultimately causal in nature, while others would say the appropriate explanation would be irreducible in terms of the agent's reasons or purposes. But can we explain a person's decision to buy one particular box of corn flakes rather then another? To assert we can seems no more than an expression of faith, for what evidence supports the claim?

On the one hand, to suppose that each time I am asked to choose a number, a causal explanation of why I picked that number can be provided, is to adhere to determinism, but to extrapolate wildly beyond available empirical data. On the other hand, to assume the choice can be explained in terms of my intentions is to be committed to the view that if we have no reason to prefer one choice to another, then we cannot choose at all. But we have no trouble making a random choice even in circumstances in which we would find it impossible, before or after, to think of any reason to prefer one of the alternatives. Indeed, if we had to postpone such a choice until we could think of a reason to prefer one alternative, our lives would come to a virtual standstill. Should I listen to this song or that one? Should I open this letter or that letter first? Should I walk home this way or that?[3] Without the ability to make random choices, we would be caught in a nightmare of indecision.

I believe we possess the ability to make random choices. We are not condemned to the fate of Buridan's Ass, the animal featured in medieval debate who died while, equally pressed by hunger and thirst, he stood motionless midway between a bundle of hay and a pail of water. What we would do in such a situation is make a random choice. Faced with equally attractive or unattractive alternatives, we are not bludgeoned into inactivity by some need for a decision principle. We simply choose. And to refer to such a random choice as either accidental or irresponsible would surely be misleading.

The British philosopher P. H. Nowell-Smith is thus mistaken when he equates a random occurrence with "an Act of God, or a miracle."[4] He even denies that such an occurrence could be an action at all, but as we have seen, a random choice is an ordinary sort of action that each of us performs frequently. Indeed, not only are random choices actions, they appear to be good candidates, although not the only ones, for membership in that class of actions we ordinarily designate as "free."

NOTES

1. A. C. MacIntyre, "Determinism," *Mind* 66, no. 261 (January 1957), p. 30.

2. A. J. Ayer, *Philosophical Essays* (New York: St. Martin's, 1963), p. 275.

3. See William James's intriguing discussion of his choice whether to walk home by Divinity Avenue or Oxford Street in "The Dilemma of Determinism," reprinted in *Essays on Faith and Morals* (Cleveland: The World, 1962), pp. 145–183.

4. P. H. Nowell-Smith, *Ethics* (Baltimore: Penguin, 1954), p. 282.

3

DOES GOD KNOW THE FUTURE?

In the Book of Deuteronomy, God says to the people of Israel, "I have put before you life and death, blessing and curse. Choose life—if you and your offspring would live . . ."[1] Did God know which option the people would choose? If so, how could their choice have been free? For if God knew they would choose life, then to have chosen death would have confuted God's knowledge—which is impossible. If God knew they would choose death, then to have chosen life would also have confuted God's knowledge. But God gave the people a genuine choice. So even God did not know how they would choose.

I find this line of argument persuasive, but many notable thinkers have believed it unsound. In what follows I shall present briefly a sampling of their objections and my replies.

Objection 1. "Just as your memory does not force the past to have happened, God's foreknowledge does not force the future to happen." So argued St. Augustine.[2]

Reply. Admittedly, my remembering that an event occurred does not cause the event's occurrence. And God's foreknowledge that an event will occur does not cause its occurrence. But if I know that an event occurred, then it is not within my power to alter its occurrence. Not only won't I alter it; I can't. Similarly, if God knows that an event will occur, then it is not within God's power to alter its occurrence. Even assuming God is all-powerful, God can only do what is logically possible, for what is logically impossible is incoherent, and an incoherent task is no task at all. Thus if an event will occur, even if God does not cause its occurrence, God is bound by logic to allow its occurrence. In short, knowledge does not cause events, but, given definitive knowledge of events, they are unavoidable.

Objection 2. "[W]e estimate the intimacy of relationship between two persons by the foreknowledge one has of the action of the other, without supposing that in either case the one or the other's freedom has thereby been endangered. So even divine foreknowledge cannot endanger freedom." So said the German theologian Friedrich Schleirmacher.[3]

Reply. We rarely claim more than strong belief about what others will do, for we realize that however likely our prediction, we may be proved wrong. But when we do possess knowledge, it is incompatible with free choice. For example, we know we all shall die. It follows that it is not within anyone's power to remain alive forever. If we knew not only *that* we would die but also when, where, and how we would die, then we could not avoid death in the known time, place, and manner. Strong beliefs can be confuted, but not knowledge.

Objection 3. "It is not true, then, that because God foreknew what would be within the power of our wills, nothing therefore lies within the power of our wills. For when he foreknew this, He did not foreknow nothing. Therefore, if He who foreknew what would lie within the power of our wills did not foreknow nothing, but something, then clearly something lies within the power of our wills even though God has foreknowledge of it." Again, St. Augustine.[4]

Reply. This line of reasoning begs the question, assuming what is supposed to be proved. If God foreknew our free choices, then they would be free. But can God foreknow our free choices? The argument I presented originally concludes that God cannot foreknow our free choices. Simply assuming the possibility of such foreknowledge carries no weight against the argument and identifies no mistake in it.

Objection 4. "[S]ince God lives in the eternal present, His knowledge transcends all movement of time and abides in the simplicity of its immediate present. It encompasses the infinite sweep of past and future, and regards all things in its simple comprehension as if they were now taking place. Thus, if you will think about the foreknowledge by which God distinguishes all things, you will rightly consider it to be not a foreknowledge of future events, but knowledge of a never changing present." So argued the Roman philosopher Boethius.[5]

Reply. We make certain choices before others. Indeed, certain choices presuppose others. For example, the choice to seek a divorce requires a prior choice to marry. Whatever is meant by the assertion that God transcends time (a murky claim), God presumably knows that we make certain choices before others. So God takes account of time. Admittedly, God is supposed to view the future as clearly as we view the present. But appeals to the clarity of God's knowledge only underscore why that knowledge is incompatible with the freedom of choices we are yet to make.

Objection 5. "[T]hough we do not know the true nature of God's knowledge . . . yet we know that . . . nothing of all existing things is hidden from Him and that His knowledge of them does not change their nature, but the possible retains its nature as a possibility. Anything in this enumeration that appears contradictory is so only owing to the structure of our knowledge, which has nothing in common with His knowledge except the name." So wrote the medieval Jewish sage Maimonides.[6]

Reply. If God's knowledge has nothing in common with human knowledge, then God's knowledge, unlike human knowledge, would not imply the truth of what is known. So God's knowledge, whatever its nature, may be compatible with free choice but only in some sense not relevant to the original argument. If we do not understand the meaning of the words we use, we cannot use them to make claims we understand.

Supposing that the argument with which I began can be sustained in the face of all criticism (and much more can be said on both sides), does it follow that God lacks omniscience?

Not if one adopts the view, which some commentators have attributed to Aristotle,[7] that statements about future choices are neither true nor false, but, at present, indeterminate. According to this view, it is not now true you will finish reading this entire book and not true you won't. Until you decide, the matter is indeterminate.

As the medieval Jewish philosopher Gersonides argued, to be omniscient is to know every true statement. Since it is not true you will finish reading the entire book and not true you won't, but true that the matter is indeterminate, an omniscient being does not know you will finish reading and does not know you won't, but does know the whole truth, namely, that the matter is indeterminate and depends on your free choice.

Thus, assuming God is omniscient, God knows the entire physical structure of the universe but not the outcome of free choices. As Gersonides wrote, "[T]he fact that God does not have the knowledge of which possible outcome will be realized does not imply any defect in God (may He be blessed). For perfect knowledge of something is the knowledge of what that thing is in reality; when the thing is not apprehended as it is, this is error, not knowledge. Hence, God knows these things in the best manner possible . . . "[8]

In other words, when God offered the people of Israel both life and death, God, although omniscient, did not know which choice they would make. God knew all that was knowable, the whole truth. But the whole truth was that the choice of life or death rested with the people of Israel. They were responsible for their decision. God awaited, but could not foresee, the outcome of their exercise of freedom.

Some may find this view unsettling, since it implies that God's knowledge, while in a sense complete, does not include within its purview definitive answers to all questions about the future. But, like Gersonides, I find this conclusion consistent with the Holy Scriptures. As Gersonides wrote, "God (may He be blessed), by means of the Prophets, commands men who are about to suffer evil fortune that they mend their ways so that they will avert this punishment. . . . Now this indicates that what God knows of future events is known by Him as not necessarily occurring."[9] In short, Divine warnings imply uncertain outcomes.

I conclude with an admission. Certain Biblical passages may suggest, contrary to what I have argued, that God knows the future in all its details, including the outcome of future free choices. If such textual evidence were presented, how would I respond? I would echo Gersonides: "If the literal sense of the Torah differs from reason, it is necessary to interpret these passages in accordance with the demands of reason."[10] The task of developing such interpretations, if required, I leave to others.

NOTES

1. *Tanakh: The Holy Scriptures* (Philadelphia: Jewish Publication Society, 1988), Deuteronomy 30:19.

2. *On Free Choice of the Will*, trans. Thomas Williams (Indianapolis: Hackett, 1993), Book III, sec. 4, p. 78.

3. *The Christian Faith*, ed. H. R. Mackintosh and J. S. Stewart (Edinburgh: T. and T. Clark, 1928), p. 228.

4. *The City of God against the Pagans*, trans. R. W. Dyson (Cambridge: Cambridge University Press, 1998), Book V, sec. 10, p. 205.

5. *The Consolation of Philosophy*, trans. Richard Green (New York: Library of Liberal Arts, 1962), Book 5, prose 6, p. 116.

6. *The Guide of the Perplexed*, trans. Chaim Rabin (Indianapolis: Hackett, 1995), p. 163.

7. See, for example, Richard Taylor, "The Problem of Future Contingencies," *The Philosophical Review* 66 (1957), pp. 1–28.

8. *The Wars of the Lord*, trans. Seymour Feldman (Philadelphia: Jewish Publication Society, 1987), vol. 2, p. 118.

9. *Ibid.* p. 118.

10. *Ibid.* p. 98.

II

BELIEF IN GOD

4

DOES GOD EXIST?

A theist believes God exists. An atheist believes God does not exist. An agnostic believes the available evidence is insufficient to decide the matter. Which of these positions is the most reasonable?

The first step in answering this question is to determine what is to be meant by the term "God." The word has been used in various ways, ranging from the Greek concept of the Olympian gods to John Dewey's concept of the "active relation between ideal and actual."[1] Let us adopt the more usual view, common to many religious believers, that "God" refers to an all-good, all-powerful, eternal Creator of the world. The question then is whether a Being of that description exits.

Throughout the centuries various arguments have been put forth to prove the existence of God. One of the best known is the cosmological argument, which rests on the assumption that everything that exists is caused to exist by something else. For example, a house is caused to exist by its builder, and rain is caused to exist by certain meteorological conditions. But if everything that exists is caused to exist by something else, then the world itself must be caused to exist by something else. This "something else" is God.

Although the cosmological argument may have an initial plausibility, a major difficulty with it is that if everything that exists is caused to exist by something else, then the cause of the world's existence is itself caused to exist by something else. In that case the cause of the world's existence is not God, for God is an all-powerful, eternal Being who does not depend on anything else for His existence. A defender of the cosmological argument might try to surmount this difficulty by claiming that the cause of the world's existence is not caused to exist by something else but is self-caused, that is, the reason for its existence lies within itself. However, if we admit the possibility that something is self-caused, the argument crumbles, for if the cause of the world's existence can be self-caused, why cannot the world be self-caused? In that case no need would arise to postulate an external cause of the world's existence, for this cause was postulated only to explain the existence of the world, and if the reason for the world's existence lies within itself, then no further explanation for its existence is required.

In a last-ditch attempt to salvage the cosmological argument, a defender might argue simply that something must have started everything, and that this "something" is God. Yet even if we grant the claim that something must have started everything (and this claim could be questioned by appealing to the mathematical notion of an infinite series), it hardly follows that the "something" is all-good, all-powerful, or eternal. Perhaps the first cause is evil, or perhaps it ceased to exist after a brief life. No such possibility are excluded by the cosmological argument, and so the argument is not successful.

A second classic proof for the existence of God is the ontological argument. This argument, which was defended by such eminent philosophers as Descartes, Spinoza, and Leibniz, makes no appeal to empirical evidence but purports to demonstrate that the very nature of God implies His existence.

The argument has various versions, but its basic structure remains the same. God is defined as a Being who possesses every perfection. It is more perfect to exist than not to exist. Thus, since God possesses every perfection, and existence is a perfection, God must exist.

Although this argument has been ably defended, it is open to the devastating criticism, stated succinctly by Kant, that existence is not an attribute. In other words, the definition of anything remains the same regardless of whether that thing exists. For example, the definition of a unicorn would not be altered if we discovered a living unicorn, just as our definition of a whooping crane would not be altered if whooping cranes became extinct. In short, whether unicorns or whooping cranes exist does not affect the meaning of the terms "unicorn" and "whooping crane."

To clarify the point, imagine a ferocious tiger. Now imagine a ferocious tiger that exists. What more is there to imagine in the second case than in the first? Our concept of a ferocious tiger remains the same whether or not any ferocious tigers exist.

Applying this insight to the ontological argument, we can see why the argument is unsound. Since the definition of a thing remains the same whether or not the thing exists, it follows that the definition of "God" remains the same whether or not He exists. Thus existence cannot be part of the definition of God. God may be defined as a Being who possesses all perfections, but existence is not a perfection, since existence is no attribute at all. To assert that something exists is not to ascribe a perfection to the thing but to state a fact about the world. What we mean by the term "God" is one matter; whether God exists is another. The ontological argument confuses the two matters and thereby goes awry.

Even if the ontological argument were sound, its abstruseness would impede its popular appeal. The next argument we shall consider, the teleological argument, is easily understood and highly plausible.

Defenders of this argument invite us to look around at the world in which we live. They point out that it possesses a highly ordered structure, just like an extraordinarily complex machine. Each part of the machine is adjusted to all the other parts with wondrous precision, and the more we investigate the working of the world, the more we are amazed at its intricate patterns. For instance, the human eye, which so many of us take for granted, is a mechanism of such enormous complexity that its design is breathtaking. But doesn't a design require a designer? The magnificent order of our world cannot be a result of pure chance, but must be the work of a Supreme Mind that is responsible for the order. That Supreme Mind is God.

Although this argument has persuasive power, it suffers from several fatal flaws. Note first that any world would exhibit some order. Were you at random to drop ten coins on the floor they would exhibit an order. An order, therefore, does not imply an orderer. If we use the term "design" to mean "a consciously established order," then a design implies a designer. But the crucial question is whether our world exhibits mere order or design.

If the world were just like a machine, as the teleological argument assumes, then since a machine has a design and a designer, so would the world. Is it obvious that the world is just like a machine? In his classic book *Dialogues Concerning Natural Religion*, Hume argues that our experience is too limited for us to accept such an analogy. Hume notes that although the world bears some slight resemblance to a machine, the world is also similar to an animal in that "[a] continual circulation of matter in it produces no disorder, a continual waste in every part is incessantly repaired; the closest sympathy is perceived throughout the entire system; and each part or member, in performing its proper offices, operates both to its own preservation and to that of the whole."[2] Hume further points out that the world is somewhat like a vegetable, since neither has sense organs or brains, although both exhibit life and movement. But whereas any machine requires a designer of the machine, animals and vegetables come into being very differently from machines. Hume does not intend to prove that the world came into being as an animal or vegetable does, but he wishes to show that the world is not sufficiently like an animal, a vegetable, or a machine to permit us to draw reasonable conclusions from such weak analogies. Lacking such an analogy, the teleological argument collapses, for we are left with no reason to believe that the world exhibits a design rather than an order.

However, as Hume pointed out, even if we were to accept the analogy the argument fails. Let us grant, he says, that like effects prove like causes. If the world is like a machine, the cause of the world is like the cause of a machine. Machines are usually built after many trials; so the world was probably built after many trials. Machines are usually built by many workers; so the world was probably built by many deities. Those who build machines are often inexperienced, careless, or foolish; so the gods, too, may be inexperienced, careless, or foolish. As Hume suggests, perhaps this world "was only the first rude essay of some infant deity, who afterwards abandoned it, ashamed of his lame performance." Or perhaps "it is the work only of some dependent, inferior deity, and is the object of derision to his superiors." It might even be "the production of old age and dotage in some superannuated deity, and ever since his death has run on at adventures, from the first impulse and active force which it received from him."[3] By suggesting such possibilities Hume demonstrates that even if we grant an analogy between the world and a machine and agree that the world was designed as a machine is designed, we are not committed to believing that the world's design is due to one all-good, all-powerful, eternal Designer.

What, then, is the source of order? The world may have gone through innumerable structural changes until a stable pattern was reached, and the existence of such complex phenomena as the human eye may be a result of the process of natural selection whereby forms of life that cannot adjust to their environment disappear, while forms of life that can adjust survive. Such an explanation of the world's order not only requires no resources to the hypothesis of a Supreme Designer but has also been confirmed by biological research since the time of Darwin.

This reply to the teleological argument may appear conclusive, but some of the argument's proponents have responded that the existence of God is not implied merely by the order in the world but, as Berkeley put it, by the "surprising magnificence, beauty, and perfection" of that order.[4] In other words, such a perfect world as the one in which we live could not possibly be either the work of an inferior deity or the outcome of impersonal natural processes. Only an all-good, all-powerful Creator could have produced such a flawless masterpiece.

This defense of the teleological argument, however, rests on the highly dubious premise that the world is perfect. In fact, the evidence against this view is overwhelming. Just consider droughts, floods, famines, hurricanes, tornadoes, earthquakes, and the innumerable varieties of disease that plague us. Is it a perfect world in which babies are born deformed, small children are bitten by rats, and young people die from leukemia? And what of the evils people cause each other? The savageries of war, the indignities of slavery, and the torments of injustice and treachery extend far beyond the limits of our imagination. In short, the human condition is of such a nature that, as Hume observed, "The man of a delicate, refined temper, by being so much more alive than the rest of the world, is only so much more unhappy."[5]

We need not go on long enumerating the ills of our world, before the teleological argument loses its last vestige of plausibility. Indeed, human misery poses a serious problem even for the theist who abandons the teleological argument; for why should we suffer evils if, as theists affirm, our world was created by an all-good, all-powerful Being? An all-good Being would do everything possible to abolish evil. An all-powerful Being would be able to abolish evil. So if an all-good, all-powerful Being existed, evil would not. But evil exists. Therefore, it would seem that an all-good, all-powerful Being doesn't.

Until this point, those who do not believe in the existence of God have been on the defensive, attempting to refute arguments that purport to prove the existence of God. Now it is those who believe in the existence of God who are on the defensive, for they must reply to the challenge known as "the problem of evil": How is it possible for evil to exist in a world created by an all-good, all-powerful Being? As Epicurus put it, is God willing to prevent evil, but not able? Then He is impotent. Is He able, but not willing? Then He is malevolent. Is He both able and willing? Whence then is evil?

Numerous attempts have been made to provide a theodicy, a defense of God's goodness in the face of evil. The most promising approach begins by distinguishing two types of evil; moral and physical. Moral evils are those for which human beings are responsible, evils such as murder, theft, and oppression. Physical evils are those for which human beings are not responsible, evils resulting from such natural phenomena as typhoons, locusts, and viruses.

Moral evils are justified by the hypothesis that God has given us free will, the power to do both good and evil. Which we do is up to us. God could have ensured that we always act rightly, but had He done so, He would have had to take away our free will, since a person who is forced to act rightly is not free. God is all-powerful, but He cannot perform an act whose description is contradictory, for such an act is no act at all. For example, since to speak of a square circle makes no sense, it is no limitation on God's ability that He cannot draw a square circle. Similarly, it is no limitation of God's ability that He cannot create free persons who must always do what is right, for, by definition, a free person is one who does not always have to do what is right. God, therefore, had to choose between creating beings who always did what was right and creating beings who were free to do both right and wrong. In His wisdom He chose the latter, since it constituted the greater good. Thus all moral evils are justified as necessary concomitants of the best possible world God could have created, namely, a world in which persons have free will.

Physical evils may be justified in one of two ways. According to one approach, physical evils provide the opportunity for human beings to develop moral attributes. If the world were a paradise without hardships and dangers, it would not be possible for people to acquire the strength of character that results from standing firm in the face of difficulties. According to this view, the world was not intended as a pleasure palace but as an arena in which human beings grapple with their weaknesses and in so doing acquire the strength that will serve them well in some future life. An alternative approach to physical evils explains them as resulting from the free actions of the Devil, whose freedom is a greater good than would be his performing right actions involuntarily.

Does this two-pronged reply to the problem of evil succeed in blunting its force? To some extent. Those who pose the problem claim that it is logically impossible that an all-good, all-powerful Being would permit the existence of evil. As we have seen, it is possible under certain circumstances that an all-good, all-powerful Being would have to allow evil to exist, for if the evil were a necessary component of the best possible world, then a Being who wished to bring about the best possible world would have to utilize whatever evil was necessary to the achievement of that goal. Thus no contradiction is involved in asserting that a world containing evil was created by an all-good, all-powerful Being.

Yet is there any reason to believe that we live in the best possible world and that all the evils are logically necessary? I would answer this question as Bertrand Russell did. He was once asked what his reaction would be if, after death, he found himself in the presence of God. Russell replied that this possibility was extremely unlikely. His questioner persisted, "What would you say to God if, contrary to all you believe, you were to find yourself in

His presence?" Russell replied, "I would tell Him He should have given us more evidence."

Those who believe in the existence of God despite the lack of such evidence may possibly be rewarded in a hereafter for their display of tenacity. But no less likely is the possibility that those who do not believe in the existence of God will be rewarded for their adherence to rationality.[6]

NOTES

1. John Dewey, *A Common Faith* (New Haven: Yale University Press, 1934), p. 51.
2. David Hume, part VI.
3. David Hume, part V.
4. George Berkeley, *A Treatise Concerning the Principles of Human Knowledge*, #146.
5. David Hume, part X.
6. The possibility of reinterpreting the concept of God within a naturalistic framework is discussed in chapter 10.

5

CACODAEMONY

For many centuries philosophers have grappled with what has come to be known as "the problem of evil." Succinctly stated, the problem is: Could a world containing evil have been created by an omnipotent, omniscient, omnibenevolent being?

Considering the vast literature devoted to this issue, it is perhaps surprising that there has been little discussion of an analogous issue that might appropriately be referred to as "the problem of goodness." Succinctly stated, the problem is: Could a world containing goodness have been created by an omnipotent, omniscient, omnimalevolent being?

This essay has two aims. The first is to provide a reasonable solution to the problem of goodness. Traditional theists find the hypothesis of creation by a benevolent deity far more plausible than the hypothesis of creation by a malevolent demon, and they may, therefore, believe the problem of goodness to be irrelevant to their commitments. My second aim is to demonstrate that this belief is mistaken.

Before proceeding, it would be well to restate the problem of goodness in more formal fashion.

1) Assume that there exists an omnipotent, omniscient, omnimalevolent Demon who created the world.
2) If the Demon exists, there would be no goodness in the world.
3) But there is goodness in the world.
4) Therefore, the Demon does not exist.

Since the conclusion of the argument follows from the premises, those who wish to deny the conclusion must deny one of the premises. No demonist (the analogue to a theist) would question premise (1), so in order to avoid the conclusion of the argument, an attack would have to be launched against either premise (2) or premise (3).

What if a demonist attempted to deny premise (3)? Suppose it were claimed that goodness is an illusion, that there is nothing of this sort in the world. Would this move solve the problem?

I think not, for such a claim is either patently false or else involves a distortion of the usual meaning of the term "good." If the word is being used in its ordinary sense, then acts of kindness, expressions of love, and creations of beauty are good. Since obviously such things do occur, there is goodness in the world.

If one insists that such things are not good, then the expression "good" is being used eccentrically, and the claim loses its import. It is as though one were to defend the view that all persons are pigs by defining "persons" as "omnivorous hoofed mammals of the family Suidae." Such "persons" are not persons at all. Similarly, a supposedly omnimalevolent Demon who cherishes personal affection and great works of art is certainly not omnimalevolent and is probably no demon.

Premise (3) can thus be adequately defended, and if demonists are to find an answer to the problem of goodness, they must attack premise (2). How can there be goodness in the world if the creator is omnimalevolent and possesses the power and the knowledge to carry out evil intentions? To paraphrase Epicurus, is the Demon willing to prevent good, but not able? Then he is impotent. Is he able, but not willing? Then he is benevolent. Is he both able and willing? Whence then is goodness?

At this point it may appear to be a hopeless task to justify the Demon's malevolence in the face of the fact of goodness, an enterprise appropriately referred to as "cacodaemony" (the analogue of theodicy). But sophisticated demonists would realize there is much play left in their position. They would not agree that just because there is goodness in the world, it could not have been created by the omnimalevolent Demon. After all, isn't it possible that whatever goodness exists is logically necessary for this to be the most evil world that the Demon could have created? Not even an omnipotent being can contravene the laws of logic, for such a task is senseless, and so if each and every good in the world were logically tied to the achievement of the greatest evil, the omnimalevolent Demon, in order to bring about the greatest possible evil, would have been forced to allow the existence of these goods.

The demonist thus rejects premise (2) of the argument and argues instead for premise (2'):

(2') If the Demon exists, then every good in the world is logically necessary in order for this to be most evil world that the Demon could
have created.

Now if we substitute premise (2') for premise (2) in the original argument,
that argument falls apart, for the conclusion no longer follows from the
premises. One can affirm without contradiction both the existence of an
omnipotent, omniscient, omnimalevolent Demon who created the world
and the existence of goodness in the world, so long as one also affirms that
every good is logically necessary in order for this to be the most evil world
the Demon could have created. Demonists thus appear to have escaped the
force of the problem of goodness.

Things are not so simple, for now demonists are faced by yet another
argument that challenges their belief.

1) Assume that there exists an omnipotent, omniscient, omnimalevolent Demon who created the world.
2) If the Demon exists, then every good in the world is logically necessary in order for this to be the most evil world that the Demon
could have created.
3) But there is strong reason to believe that not every good in the world
is logically necessary in order for this to be the most evil world the
Demon could have created.
4) Therefore, there is strong reason to believe that the Demon does
not exist.

This second argument, unlike the first, does not claim that belief in
the Demon is illogical; rather, it claims that such belief is unreasonable.
Beautiful mountain ranges, spectacular sunsets, the plays of Shakespeare,
and the quartets of Beethoven do not seem in any way to enhance the evils
of the world. Acts of altruism, generosity, and kindheartedness certainly do
not appear to increase the world's sinister aspects. In other words, this argument challenges demonists to suggest plausible reasons for their view
that every good in the world makes possible a world containing even
greater evils than would be possible without these goods.

The reader will, of course, have observed that thus far the discussion of
the problem of goodness exactly parallels traditional discussions of the problem of evil; all the arguments and counterarguments that have been presented are equally applicable *mutatis mutandis* to either problem. What may
be somewhat surprising, however, is that classic arguments in defense of the

view that every evil in the world makes possible a world containing even greater goods can be exactly paralleled by arguments in defense of the view that every good in the world makes possible a world containing even greater evils. To illustrate this point, I shall proceed to construct a cacodaemony along the identical lines of the well-known theodicy constructed by John Hick.[1]

We begin by dividing all goods into two sorts: moral goods and physical goods. Moral goods are those human beings do for each other; physical goods are those to be found in the human environment.

The justification of moral goods proceeds by logically tying the existence of such goods to human free will. Surely, performing a bad act freely is more evil than performing such an act involuntarily. The Demon could have ensured that human beings would always perform bad actions, but such actions would not have been free, since the Demon would have ensured their occurrence.[2] Because the actions would not have been free, their performance would not have produced the greatest possible evil, since greater evil can be produced by free persons than by unfree ones. The Demon, therefore, had to provide human beings with freedom, so that they might perform their bad actions voluntarily, thus maximizing evil.

As for the justification of physical goods, we should not suppose that the Demon's purpose in creating the world was to construct a mere chamber of tortures in which the inhabitants would be forced to endure a succession of unrelieved pains. The world can be viewed, instead, as a place of "soul-breaking," in which free human beings, by grappling with the exhausting tasks and challenges of their existence in a common environment, can thereby have their spirits broken and their wills-to-live destroyed.[3]

This conception of the world can be supported by what, following Hick, we may call "the method of negative cacodaemony."[4] Suppose, contrary to fact, that this world were arranged so that nothing could ever go well. No one could help anyone else, no one could perform a courageous act, no one could complete any worthwhile project. Presumably, such a world could be created through innumerable acts of the Demon that would continually alter the laws of nature as necessary.

It is evident that our present ethical concepts would be useless in such a world, for "ought" implies "can," and if no good acts could be performed, it would follow that none ought to be performed. The whole notion of "evil" would seem to drop out, for to understand and recognize evils we must have some idea of goods. Consequently, such a world, however efficiently it might promote pains, would be ill-adapted for the development of the worst qualities of the human personality.

At this point, this cacodaemony, just as Hick's theodicy, points forward in two ways to the subject of life after death. First, although there are many striking instances of evil being brought forth from good through a person's reaction to it (witness the pollution of beautiful lakes or the slashing of great paintings), still there are many other cases in which the opposite has happened. Therefore it would seem that any demonic purpose of soul-breaking at work in earthly history must continue beyond this life if it is ever to achieve more than a very partial and fragmentary success.[5]

Second, if we ask whether the business of soul-breaking is so evil as to nullify all the goodness to be found in human life, the demonist's answer must be in terms of a future evil great enough to justify all that has happened on the way to it.[6]

Have we now provided an adequate cacodaemony? It is, I think, just as strong as Hick's theodicy, but neither in my view is successful. Nor do I see any plausible ways of strengthening either one. What reason is there to believe in an afterlife of any particular sort? What evidence is there that the world would be either better without the beauty of a sunset or worse without the horrors of bubonic plague? What evidence is there either that the free will of a Socrates achieved greater evil than would have been achieved by his performing wrong actions involuntarily or that the free will of a Hitler achieved greater good than would have been achieved by his performing right actions involuntarily?

The hypothesis that all the good in the world is a necessary part of this worst of all possible worlds is not contradictory; nevertheless, it is highly unlikely. Similarly, the hypothesis that all the evil in the world is a necessary part of this best of all possible worlds is not contradictory; but it, too, is highly unlikely. If this is neither the worst of all possible worlds nor the best of all possible worlds, then it could not have been created by either an all-powerful, all-evil demon or an all-powerful, all-good diety. Thus although the problem of goodness and the problem of evil do not show either demonism or theism to be impossible views, they show them both to be highly improbable. If demonists or theists can produce any other evidence in favor of their positions, they may be able to increase the plausibility of their views, but unless they can produce such evidence, the reasonable conclusion appears to be that neither the Demon nor God exists.

NOTES

1. See his *Philosophy of Religion, 2nd Edition* (Englewood Cliffs, N.J.: Prentice-Hall, 1975), pp. 36–43.

2. I here assume without argument that freedom and determinism are incompatible. Those who believe they are not face more difficulty in resolving the problem of goodness (or the problem of evil).

3. Hick sees the world as a place of "soul making," in which free beings grapple with the challenges of their existence and may thereby become "children of God."

4. Hick refers to "the method of negative theodicy," which supposes that the world is arranged without pain or suffering.

5. Hick says the same for "any divine purpose of soul making."

6. Hick appeals to "a future good great enough" to serve as such a justification.

6

THE MORIARTY HYPOTHESIS

Why does an all-powerful, all-knowing, all-good God allow evil? Theists who seek to answer this question may take comfort in firmly embracing a justification that accommodates all past, present, and future evils, however horrific. But this approach leads to a philosophical pitfall.

To see why, consider the fictional example of Sherlock Holmes and his archfiend, Professor Moriarty. Holmes believed that Moriarty was the "great malignant brain" behind crime in London, the "deep organizing power" that unified "every deviltry" into "one connected whole," the "foul spider which lurks in the centre," "never caught—never so much as suspected."[1] Now suppose Moriarty's power extended throughout the universe, so that all events (perhaps excluding acts of human freedom) were the work of one omnipotent, omniscient, omnimalevolent demon. Let us call this theory "the Moriarty hypothesis."

Does the presence of various goods refute the Moriarty hypothesis? No, for just as theism can be shown to be logically consistent with the world's most horrendous evils, so the Moriarty hypothesis can be shown to be logically consistent with the world's most wonderful goods. While evils can be viewed as logically necessary for the greater good, goods can be viewed as logically necessary for the greater evil.[2]

Assuming, then, that the Moriarty hypothesis is not obviously false and leaving aside speculation about whether a next life may bring greater goods or greater evils, do theists have any different expectations about the events of this life than do those who accept the Moriarty hypothesis?

39

Consider the following two assessments of the human condition:

1) "[I]s not all life pathetic and futile? . . . We reach. We grasp. And what is left in our hands at the end? A shadow. Or worse than a shadow—misery."
2) "The first entrance into life gives anguish to the new-born infant and to its wretched parent; weakness, impotence, distress attend each stage of that life, and it is at last finished in agony and horror."

Which is the viewpoint of a theist and which that of a believer in the Moriarty hypothesis? As it happens, (1) is uttered by Sherlock Holmes,[3] (2) by the orthodox believer Demea in Part X of *Hume's Dialogues Concerning Natural Religion*. The positions appear interchangeable.

Both the theist and the believer in the Moriarty hypothesis recognize that life contains happiness as well as misery. No matter how terrible the misery, the theist may regard it as unsurprising; after all, aren't all evils, in principle, explicable? To believers in the Moriarty hypothesis, happiness may be regarded as unsurprising; after all, aren't all goods, in principle, explicable? Supporters of both positions are apt to view events that appear to conflict with their fundamental principles merely as tests of fortitude, opportunities to display strength of commitment.

If defenders of either view modified their beliefs in the light of changing circumstances, then their expectations would differ. But believers are loath to admit doubt. They admire those who stand fast in their faith, regardless of appearances.

Any seemingly contrary evidence can be considered ambiguous. St. Paul says, "we see in a mirror, dimly,"[4] and Sherlock Holmes speaks of seeking the truth "through the veil which shrouded it."[5] If events are so difficult to interpret, they provide little reason for believers to abandon deep-seated tenets. Those who vacillate are typically viewed by other members of their communities as weakhearted and faithless.

One other attempt to differentiate the expectations of the theist and the believer in the Moriarty hypothesis is to suppose that theists have reason to be more optimistic than their counterparts. But this presumption is unwarranted. Recall the words from the Book of Ecclesiastes: "I accounted those who died long since more fortunate than those who are still living; and happier than either are those who have not yet come into being and have never witnessed the miseries that go on under the sun."[6] A more pessimistic view is hard to imagine.

We may be living, as the theist supposes, in the best of all possible worlds, but, if so, the best of all possible worlds contains immense torments. On the other hand, we may be living, as the believer in the Moriarty hypothesis supposes, in the worst of all possible worlds, but, if so, the worst of all possible worlds contains enormous delights. Both scenarios offer us reason to be cheerful and reason to be gloomy. Our outlook depends on our personalities, not our theology or demonology.

So, as we seek to understand life's vicissitudes, does it make any difference whether we believe in God or in the Moriarty hypothesis? Not if we hold either of these beliefs unshakeably. For the more tenaciously we cling to one of them, the less it matters which one.

NOTES

1. *The Complete Sherlock Holmes* (Garden City, N.Y.: Doubleday, n.d.), pp. 471, 496, 769. The works cited are "The Final Problem," "The Adventure of the Norwood Builder," and "The Valley of Fear."

2. See my "Cacodaemony," *Analysis* 37 (1977), pp. 69–73 (chapter 5 in this book).

3. See "The Adventure of the Retired Colourman," p. 1113.

4. I Corinthians 13:12.

5. See "The Final Problem," p. 471.

6. Ecclesiastes 4:2, 3. The translation is from *Tanakh: The Holy Scriptures* (Philadelphia: Jewish Publication Society, 1988).

7

JOB'S PROTEST

Certain works of literature have inspired such voluminous commentary that first-time readers may possess a preconceived notion of the author's intention and may interpret what they read so as to bear out their preconception. So it is with the Book of Job. I want to show that the accepted interpretation of the work is, in fact, belied by a straightforward reading of the text.

Consider the plot. After a short introduction in which Job's exemplary piety and extraordinary good fortune are described, the scene shifts to heaven, where a dialogue takes place between God and Satan. God proudly comments to Satan concerning Job's great spiritual qualities. Satan scoffs at Job's devoutness, claiming that Job is obedient only because God has given Job good health, a fine family, and untold wealth. Although God Himself testifies to Job's genuine piety, He permits Satan to test Job by inflicting on him the severest personal losses. All ten of Job's children die suddenly, and his wealth is destroyed. When Job does not relinquish his faith in God, Satan, claiming that Job has maintained his faith only because his own body has been spared, obtains further permission from God to inflict on Job a most painful disease.

The scene now shifts permanently to earth, in the land of Uz, the place of Job's residence. Having heard of his misfortunes, Job's three friends, Eliphaz, Bildad, and Zophar, come to comfort him. Job then gives vent to his feelings of despair; he curses the day he was born, crying that death is better than life under his circumstances. Eliphaz advises Job to calm himself and not despise the chastening of the Almighty. Eliphaz believes that since Job is suffering, Job must have sinned, for God does not punish the innocent. Eliphaz counsels Job to repent of his sins, and so be restored to God's favor.

Job points out that Eliphaz has not understood Job's outburst. Job has not lost faith in God. Rather, Job longs for death because life has become impossible. "Why does He give light to the sufferer/And light to the bitter in spirit; To those who wait for death but it does not come."[1] In a harsh rejoinder, Bildad tells Job that God does not pervert justice, and that if Job were upright he would be prosperous. Job once again pleads with his friends that they do not understand the point of his complaint. He recognizes, as they do, the majesty of God, but Job claims to be innocent. He only wishes to know in what way he has erred, so that he might wholeheartedly repent. He finally cries to God that he would willingly present his case before Him, if the Almighty would only permit him the opportunity.

The three friends and a newcomer, Elihu, repeat Eliphaz's basic argument: Job is suffering and, therefore, is a sinner; if he would repent of his sins, God would pardon him. Some scholars find different emphases in each of these four speakers, one representing man's reliance on the wisdom of God, another representing man's reliance on the power of God, and so forth.[2] In any case, Job's position remains the same. Although he speaks with moving appeal on a variety of subjects, including his disappointment in his friends, the wearisomeness and brevity of life, the insignificance of humanity, and the greatness of God, his essential idea is that, although he claims innocence, he is prepared to be judged, and, if found guilty, stands ready to accept just punishment.

The climax of the story comes when God answers Job from out of a whirlwind. God speaks of His own wisdom and power in the creation and control of the mighty forces of nature. "Have you ever commanded the day to break,/Assigned the dawn its place."[3] He points out the utter insignificance of humanity in the presence of God. "Is it by your wisdom that the hawk grows pinions,/Spreads his wings to the south?/Does the eagle soar at your command, Building his nest high."[4] He questions Job's right even to inquire of God, since how could humanity ever hope to understand the workings of the Almighty? Finally, he urges Job to renew his faith in the wisdom, goodness and justice of God, even though Job cannot hope to understand their workings.

Job is overawed. He humbles himself before God, promising never to inquire of God again but forever to believe fervently in the greatness and power of the Lord. The story concludes as God rebukes Eliphaz, Bildad, and Zophar for the advice they gave Job, pardoning them only out of regard for him. Lastly, He heals Job, restores to him twice as much wealth as he had possessed before his misfortunes, and blesses him with ten children and a long and happy life.

Now let us examine the traditional interpretation of the Book. In its most simple and direct form, it is this:

"The Book of Job teaches us that God's ways are beyond the complete understanding of our little minds. Like Job, we must believe that God, who placed us in this world, knows what is best for us. Such faith in the goodness of God, even though we cannot altogether understand it, brings us strength and confidence to face our calamities, and sorrows and sufferings."[5]

As set forth by the great medieval Jewish philosopher, Moses Maimonides, it is this:

"In the same manner, as there is a difference between works of nature and productions of human handicraft, so there is a difference between God's rule, providence, and intention in reference to all natural forces, and our rule, providence, and intention in reference to things which are the objects of our rule, providence, and intention. This lesson is the principal object of the whole Book of Job; it lays down its principle of faith, and recommends us to derive a proof from nature, that should not fall into the error of imagining His knowledge to be similar to ours. . . ."[6]

As explained by a contemporary Jewish thinker, the interpretation is this:

"The total mystery of God can be gleaned from the Book of Job. There we are presented with a deity whose workings in nature can in no way be inferred from a knowledge of nature's order. For how did that order come into existence? That is God's secret. Nor can man's moral intuitions be trusted. Job *knows* he is innocent, yet in the end he is satisfied to accept the dictate that the conventional-minded friends with whom he has carried on a courageous, honest debate are in a sense correct. Who is he, a mere mortal, to challenge God's justice? There is infinitely more to it than even his clear conscience can hope to fathom. Indeed he cannot any longer allow himself to think of God as just or unjust, at least as these terms are understood by man. These categories have no meaning when applied to God."[7]

As stated by Samuel Terrien in one of the leading modern Christian commentaries on the Bible, it is this:

"With a keen sense of drama and a profound knowledge of psychology, the poet withholds until the climax of his work the secret of his intention, which is to show the divinity of God, the humanity of man, and the specific nature of the relation between a God who is truly God and a man who is truly man—namely, one of grace apprehended by faith."[8]

As presented by Aage Bentzen, a leading European Christian theologian, it is this:

> "... the book does not give a theoretical solution of the problem of retribution, but on the basis of the experience of the poet it points out that the solution is to be found in the practical religious position, in which everything, doubts and defiance and desperate longing, may be freely expressed in words, and in which the meeting with the Almighty assures man of God's trustworthiness, an assurance being 'the substance of things hoped for, the evidence of things not seen.' The book thus proclaims the decisive signification of *faith* for the understanding of man and God."[9]

As proposed by David Trueblood, an American philosopher of religion, it is this:

> "The positive contribution of the *Book of Job* comes in the 'Speeches of the Lord' which give Job something better than that which is provided by the feeble remarks of his friends. The essential point of these final speeches is that the problem is too great for the finite mind, that Job sees only a small segment of reality, and that his criticisms are accordingly inappropriate. How can Job *know* that either God's power or goodness is limited? His knowledge of temporal things is admittedly slight; his knowledge of eternal things is still more slight. The conclusion of the book is Job's recognition of his own humble status with the consequent mood of childlike trust."[10]

Finally, according to Marvin Pope in his introduction to the *Anchor Bible* edition of *Job*, it is this:

> "The one final reality appears to be the process by which things come into being, exist, and pass away. This ultimate Force, the Source and End to all things, is inexorable. Against it there is no defense. Any hope a man may put in anything other than this First and Last One is vain. There is nothing else that abides. This is God. . . . The transition from fear and hatred to trust and even love of this One—from God the Enemy to God the Friend and Companion—is the pilgrimage of every man of faith. Job's journey from despair to faith is the way each mortal must go."[11]

All the various forms of the one basic interpretation overlook a key passage: the opening dialogue in heaven. If this scene were eliminated, the traditional interpretation would be persuasive. Readers would be in the place of Job. They would not know why he was suffering, and would, like Job, be overawed by God's appearance from out of the whirlwind.

But readers are not in this position. They were told explicitly at the outset of the story why Job was going to suffer. Satan had, in effect, made a wager with God as to the strength of Job's faith, and the wager required Job's suffering. God's words from out of the whirlwind at the climax of the plot appear childish when one is, in effect, "behind the scenes." For God to have answered Job's question truthfully would have shown Him to be anything but a great moral force. Does a righteous being make a wager involving human lives? So, much in the manner of the bully who, when engaged in a philosophical dispute, challenges his opponents to a fistfight in order to settle the issue, God attacks Job's position *ad hominem*, trying to disallow Job's right to ask an embarrassing question by indicating his inability to control nature.

Job does not possess God's power, but Job's question remains unanswered. Job may be overawed, but readers should not be, for they are aware of the circumstances surrounding God's actions. God's ways may be beyond Job's understanding, but they are not beyond the readers'. One can hardly be expected to have "childlike trust" in the goodness of a God who not only punishes Job unfairly but kills his ten children without any possible justification. Had these individuals done anything unjust? Their lives were sacrificed as part of the wager. The ten children who are given to Job at the end of the story may to a small extent compensate Job for his previous losses, but are the dead children compensated? Are they restored to life?

What, then, is the significance of the Book of Job? It should be classified as literature of revolt, in that it stands opposed to the prevailing theology of practically all the rest of the Bible. The doctrine of retributive justice, as presented in Deuteronomy, Psalms, Proverbs, and elsewhere, states that a pious person will be rewarded with wealth and happiness; a sinner will suffer both economic and physical adversity. Orthodox believers supposed that the righteous were favored by God with material rewards, and sinners were punished with calamity. The Book of Job is a criticism of this theology, a protest unique in the Bible. Later theologians, however, could not accept this protest. They tried to torture the text into the pattern of orthodox thought. In effect, they turned a challenge to the righteousness of God's justice into a defense of unquestioning faith.

The Book of Job does not justify God's ways; rather, it doubts God's goodness. It is not a book that supports faith but one that supports skepticism about faith.

NOTES

1. 3:20–21. The translation is from *Tanakh: The Holy Scriptures* (Philadelphia: Jewish Publication Society, 1988).

2. Moses Maimonides, *The Guide for The Perplexed*, translated by M. Friedlander (London: George Routledge & Sons, 1928), pp. 299–303.

3. 38:12.

4. 39:26, 27.

5. Mortimer J. Cohen, *Pathways through the Bible* (Philadelphia: Jewish Publication Society of America, 1946), p. 460.

6. Moses Maimonides, p. 303.

7. Jack J. Cohen, *The Case for Religious Naturalism* (New York: Reconstructionist Press, 1958), p. 83.

8. "Job," *The Interpreter's Bible* (1954 ed.), vol. 3, p. 898.

9. Aage Bentzen, *Introduction to the Old Testament* (Copenhagen: G. E. C. Gad, 1958), vol. II, p. 178.

10. David Trueblood, *The Logic of Belief* (New York: Harper & Brothers, 1942), pp. 293–294.

11. "Job," *The Anchor Bible* (New York: Doubleday, 1965), p. lxxvii.

8

THE NOES HAVE IT:
HUME'S *DIALOGUES*

In *Jumpers*, a play by the contemporary British dramatist Tom Stoppard, the central character, a professor of moral philosophy, reflects on the position of an atheist: "Well, the tide is running his way, and it is a tide which has turned only once in human history. . . . There is presumably a calendar date—a *moment*—when the onus of proof passed from the atheist to the believer, when, quite suddenly, secretly, the noes had it."[1] I would propose as that moment the posthumous publication in 1779 of David Hume's *Dialogues Concerning Natural Religion*.

"Natural religion" was the term used by eighteenth-century writers to refer to theological tenets provable by reason without appeal to revelation. And the three participants in the *Dialogues* are distinguished by their views concerning the scope and limits of reason. Cleanthes claims he can present arguments that demonstrate the truth of traditional Christian theology. Demea is committed to that theology but does not believe empirical evidence can provide any defense for his faith. Philo doubts that reason yields conclusive results in any field of inquiry and is especially critical of theological dogmatism.

What is the central theme of the book? The answer is not obvious, for the *Dialogues* is a work of fiction, an account offered by one literary character, Pamphilus, to another, Hermippus, of a discussion Pamphilus says he heard one summer day at the home of his teacher Cleanthes. And, as in any sophisticated drama, we are not simply told the point, we are shown it.

Some lessons, however, are obvious. The most widely-used arguments for the existence of God are subjected to trenchant criticisms. In particular, the claim that the structure of the world provides clear evidence of God's handiwork, the so-called "teleological argument," is shown to lack cogency.

But Hume not only undermines arguments for the existence of God but also develops in detail what is perhaps the strongest argument against the existence of God, namely, the problem of evil: how is it possible for evil to exist in a world created by an all-good, all-powerful God? No glib dismissal of this perplexing problem can survive a careful reading of Hume's work.

But more is going on in the *Dialogues* than an examination of arguments for and against the existence of God. Indeed, the three central characters agree that "the question can never be concerning the *being* but only the *nature* of the Deity." Yet how is it possible to make sense of the view that something exists, if all its attributes are unknown?

Suppose, for instance, you are asked whether you believe in the existence of a snark. You will inquire what a snark is, what characteristics it possesses. If you are told its nature is indescribable, what would be the sense of your affirming or denying its existence? About what would you be talking? Anyone who believes in the existence of a snark but can say nothing whatever about its nature is fundamentally confused.

The same is true of anyone who believes in the existence of God but can say nothing about God's nature. Such belief is empty. The initial agreement among Cleanthes, Demea, and Philo that God exists is thus of no significance, unless they come to some understanding of God's nature.

But they cannot do so, for when the traditional arguments for the existence of God have been shown to afford no understanding of the Divine, and the problem of evil forces the believer to seek refuge in God's incomprehensibility, theism loses its meaning. And I consider that insight the underlying theme of the *Dialogues*.

Hume's genius is demonstrated in the development of this motif, for by subtle and realistic interplay among his three main characters, he brings to light the surprising affinity between the skeptic and the person of faith, as well as the equally surprising lack of affinity between the person of faith and the philosophical theist.

For example, at the opening of Part II Demea states that God's nature is "altogether incomprehensible and unknown to us." Philo agrees and speaks of "the adorably mysterious and incomprehensible nature of the Supreme Being." Cleanthes, however, recognizes that these views render theism vacuous, and so he immediately launches into a statement of the teleological argument, thereby attempting to provide some understanding of the ways of God. Cleanthes' conclusion is that "the Author of nature is somewhat similar to the mind of man . . ."

But when Philo criticizes Cleanthes' analogy, Demea, who is suspicious of any attempt to describe the Supreme Being, sides with Philo, arguing that "the infirmities of our nature do not permit us to reach any ideas which in the least correspond to the ineffable sublimity of the Divine attributes." Cleanthes warns Demea that if he persists in maintaining that God is completely unknowable, he will rob theism of any sense, but Demea does not grasp this point and, with Philo's encouragement, continues to defend his self-defeating position.

In Part IX after Philo has completed his ferocious attack on Cleanthes' version of the argument from design, Demea suggests they rely on the cosmological argument, the claim that since whatever exists is caused to exist by something else, the ultimate cause of the entire causal chain must be God.

By placing this argument in the mouth of Demea, Hume emphasizes that even the most ardent partisans of faith must have recourse to reason if they are to defend their position. Furthermore, Hume is suggesting that those who affirm the incomprehensibility of God do not quite mean what they say, since they are prepared to try to offer some description of the Divine, even if it be so abstract a one as "necessarily existent Being . . . which determined *something* to exist rather than *nothing*."

Demea's argument is initially undermined not by Philo but by Cleanthes, who argues that the phrase "necessary existence" has no meaning and that, furthermore, no sense can be given to the notion of a first cause that is supposed to stand apart from the entire causal chain. Cleanthes' willingness to deny significance to Demea's concept of God serves as a reminder that anyone who enters the arena of reason is subject to attack by all those committed to rationality, be they theists or atheists.

In Part X where the subject of discussion turns to the evils in the world, Cleanthes again finds himself opposing Philo and Demea, both of whom defend the view that "the whole earth . . . is cursed and polluted." Cleanthes realizes that Philo can utilize the ills of the world to discredit the existence of a God who is all-good and all-powerful, but Demea fails to appreciate this difficulty, since he is confident that present evils will be rectified at some other time and place.

Cleanthes, however, is appalled by this line of reasoning, since it amounts to nothing more than an attempt to explain away the damaging evidence of evil by appealing to an arbitrary supposition about an unknown afterlife. Cleanthes understands, as Demea does not, that to take a leap of faith in the face of strong evidence to the contrary raises serious doubts about the very meaningfulness of one's faith.

If God's love for humanity is compatible with our being forced to endure the most terrible miseries, then what exactly is the significance of the claim that God loves us? How would things be different if He didn't?

Cleanthes attempts to defend the goodness of the world, hoping thereby to bolster the theistic position he and Demea share. But Philo, using evidence in part originally supplied by Demea, easily overwhelms Cleanthes, and Demea finally realizes that his apparent ally through much of the discussion has all along been his most dangerous enemy.

In Part XII, after Demea has become upset and left the company, Philo tries to soothe the displeasure exhibited by his host, Cleanthes. Many commentators have found this section puzzling, since Philo proceeds to agree with Cleanthes that the universe exhibits purpose. But the reader should have become aware by this point that Philo's apparently theistic utterances are not all they may seem to be, and Philo soon reveals the insignificance of his admission.

In the end he adopts the view that the whole of natural religion is reducible to one proposition: "*That the cause or causes of order in the universe probably bear some remote analogy to human intelligence.*" But since the import of this statement is negated by such qualifications as "cause or causes," "probably," and "remote analogy," the claim is at bottom neither theistic nor atheistic but simply devoid of clear sense. We are left only with Philo's observation that the proposition "affords no inference that affects human life . . ." And this conclusion sounds the death knell for theology.

In the final sentence of the book we are told that "Philo's principles are more probable than Demea's, but that those of Cleanthes approach still nearer to the truth." Those who assume this summation to be Hume's own find it perplexing, since so many of Cleanthes' arguments have been undermined throughout the work. However, the statement is not Hume's but that of the narrator Pamphilus, who, as a student of Cleanthes, understandably finds Cleanthes' position the most persuasive of the three.

But why should Hume have ended the *Dialogues* with a misleading assessment of the discussion? A major part of the answer is that eighteenth-century English society did not take kindly to attacks on traditional theological tenets, and, since Hume had no desire to precipitate a scandal, he adopted the literary device of a narrator who both at the beginning and the end could assure suspicious readers that, regardless of what might appear to happen in the *Dialogues*, theism is triumphant.

Indeed, Hume's friends were so fearful of the public's disapproval that, despite his precautions, they dissuaded him from publishing the manuscript. Fortunately, he took great pains to assure the work would not be lost, and it appeared in print three years after his death, although without any publisher's name attached.

Another factor that may have affected Hume's choice of an ending for the book is to be found in the work that most strongly influenced it. Although present-day readers are apt to associate the dialogue form with Plato, the model for Hume's work was not of Greek but of Roman origin. Hume was an admirer of the orator, statesman, and philosopher Cicero, who approximately eighteen hundred years before had authored a treatise on theology titled *De Natura Deorum* (*Of the Nature of the Gods*).

The parallels between the two works are striking. *De Natura Deorum* takes the form of an imaginary conversation among Velleius the Epicurean, Balbus the Stoic, and Cotta the Skeptic. All participants agree that the subject of discussion is to be not the being but the nature of the gods. Velleius argues that, although the gods exist, our senses can provide no knowledge of their essence. Balbus, on the other hand, offers what he considers scientific proofs for the existence of the gods, including a form of the teleological argument. Cotta demonstrates both the emptiness of Velleius' position and the weaknesses of each proof Balbus offers, especially the teleological argument. Cotta ends the work by presenting in detail a compelling version of the problem of evil. Although the Skeptic clearly appears to have had the best of the discussion, in the last sentence of the book Cicero states that in his view the reasoning of Balbus the Stoic more nearly approaches the truth. Cicero was himself allied with skepticism, but he preferred to close by adopting the stance of a believer, and Hume, following Cicero, decided to have his narrator Pamphilus do likewise. Perhaps both authors sensed that prudence dictated moderation in their conclusions.

An intriguing, additional feature of the comparison between the two works is that the second head of the Stoic school was named Cleanthes. And the leading exponent of skepticism in Cicero's time, the teacher who most strongly influenced his philosophical development, was named Philo. Thus did Hume pay tribute to Cicero.

How important a work is the *Dialogues Concerning Natural Religion*? Suffice it to say that never before or since has traditional Christian theology faced a more dangerous philosophical attack. And readers of the *Dialogues* are invited to listen to the conversation and judge for themselves whether that theology can be plausibly defended in the face of such a brilliant and profound challenge.

NOTE

1. *Jumpers* (New York: Grove Press, 1972), p. 25.

9

SUPPOSE GOD EXISTS

For centuries philosophers have discussed the merits of the ontological, cosmological, and teleological arguments for believing in God. Let us, however, temporarily bypass these debates and assume that some versions of these arguments make it reasonable to believe in the existence of the most perfect conceivable Being, the all-good creator of the universe. What implications follow that would be relevant to our lives?

Most persons, either out of fear or respect, would wish to act in accord with God's will. None of the arguments for believing in God, however, provides any hint whatever as to which actions God wishes us to perform or what we ought to do to please or obey Him. We may affirm that God is all-good and yet have no way of knowing the highest moral standards. All we may presume is that, whatever these standards. God always acts in accordance with them. We might expect God to have implanted the correct moral intuitions in our minds, but this supposition is doubtful in view of the conflicts among people's intuitions. And even if some consensus prevailed, it might be only a means by which God tests us to see whether we have the courage to dissent from popular opinion.

Some would argue that, if God exists, then at least it follows that murder is immoral, since it would be immoral to destroy what God in His infinite wisdom created. This argument, however, fails on several grounds. First, God also created germs, viruses, and disease-carrying rats. Does it follow that since God created these things they ought not be eliminated? Second, if God arranged for us to live, He also arranged for us to die. Does it follow that by committing murder we are assisting the work of God? Third, God provided us with the mental and physical capacities to commit murder. Does it follow that God wishes us to commit murder?

Clearly, the attempt to deduce moral precepts from God's existence is but another case of trying to do what Hume long ago pointed out to be logically impossible, *viz.*, the deduction of normative judgments from purely factual premises (*Treatise of Human Nature* III.1.1). No such deduction is valid and, thus, any moral principle is consistent with the existence of God.

Since the arguments for believing in God afford no means of distinguishing good from evil, no person can be sure how to obey God and do what is best in His eyes. We may hope our actions are in accord with God's standards, but no test is available to check. Some seemingly good persons suffer great ills, and some seemingly evil persons achieve great happiness. Perhaps in a future life these outcomes are reversed, but we have no way of ascertaining who, if anyone, is ultimately punished and who ultimately rewarded.

Holy books may be thought to provide such insights. But while many such books claim to embody the will of God, they conflict with one another. Which is to be believed? Which moral code is to be followed? Which prayers are to be recited? Which rituals are to be performed? Believing that God exists does not yield answers to these crucial questions.

Does God wish us to worship or serve Him? Perhaps, but perhaps not. Who knows what God wills? Might He not disapprove of all religious activity? Persons may devote themselves to the adoration of God, but He might look with more favor on those dedicated to quite different ends.

Orthodox believers traditionally proclaim that God is incomprehensible, inscrutable, beyond our powers of understanding. So be it. How, then, can we draw any implications from God's existence?

I conclude, as Hume apparently did at the end of his *Dialogues Concerning Natural Religion*, that the existence of God "affords no inference that affects human life."

10

RELIGION WITHOUT GOD

Most of us suppose that all religions are akin to the one we happen to know best. But this assumption can be misleading. For example, many Christians believe that all religions place heavy emphasis on an afterlife, although the central concern of Judaism is life in this world, not the next. Similarly, many Christians and Jews are convinced that a person who is religious must affirm the existence of a supernatural God. They are surprised to learn that religions such as Jainism or Theravada Buddhism deny the existence of a Supreme Creator of the world.

How can there be a nonsupernatural religion? To numerous theists as well as atheists, the concept appears contradictory. I propose to show, however, that nothing in the theory or practice of religion—not ritual, not prayer, not metaphysical belief, not moral commitment—necessitates a commitment to traditional theism. In other words, one may be religious while rejecting supernaturalism.

Let us begin with the concept of ritual. A ritual is a prescribed symbolic action. In the case of religion, the ritual is prescribed by the religious organization, and the act symbolizes some aspect of religious belief. Those who find the beliefs of supernaturalistic religion unreasonable or the activities of the organization unacceptable may come to consider any ritual irrational. Yet although particular rituals may be based on irrational beliefs, nothing is inherently irrational about ritual.

Consider the simple act of two people shaking hands when meeting. This act is a ritual, prescribed by our society and symbolic of the individuals' mutual respect. The act is in no way irrational. Of course, if people shook hands in order to ward off evil demons, then shaking hands would be irrational. But that is not the reason people shake hands. The ritual has no connection with God or demons but indicates the attitude one person has toward another.

It might be assumed that the ritual of handshaking escapes irrationality only because the ritual is not prescribed by any specific organization and is not part of an elaborate ceremony. To see that this assumption is false, consider the graduation ceremony at a college. The graduates and faculty members all wear peculiar hats and robes, and the participants stand and sit at appropriate times. However, the ceremony is not at all irrational. Indeed, the rites of graduation day, far from being irrational, are symbolic of commitment to the process of education and the life of reason.

At first glance, rituals may seem a comparatively insignificant feature of life; yet they are a pervasive and treasured aspect of human experience. Who would want to eliminate the festivities associated with holidays such as Independence Day or Thanksgiving? What would college football be without songs, cheers, flags, and the innumerable other symbolic features surrounding the game? Those who disdain popular rituals typically proceed to establish their own distinctive ones, ranging from characteristic habits of dress to the use of drugs, symbolizing a rejection of traditional mores.

Religious persons, like all others, search for an appropriate means of emphasizing their commitment to a group or its values. Rituals provide such a means. Granted, supernaturalistic religion has often infused its rituals with superstition, but nonreligious rituals can be equally as superstitious as religious ones. For instance, most Americans view the Fourth of July as an occasion on which they can express pride in their country's heritage. With this purpose in mind, the holiday is one of great significance. However, if the singing of the fourth verse of "The Star-Spangled Banner" four times on the Fourth of July were thought to protect our country against future disasters, then the original meaning of the holiday would soon be lost in a maze of superstition.

A naturalistic (i.e., nonsupernaturalistic) religion need not utilize ritual in a superstitious manner, for such a religion does not employ rituals to please a benevolent deity or to appease an angry one. Rather, naturalistic religion views rituals, as one of its exponents has put it, as "the enhancement of life through the dramatization of great ideals."[1] If a group places great stress on justice or freedom, why should it not utilize ritual in order to emphasize these goals? Such a use of ritual serves to solidify the group and to strengthen its devotion to its expressed purposes. These are strengthened all the more if the ritual in question has the force of tradition, having been performed by many generations who have belonged to the same group and have struggled to achieve the same goals. Ritual so conceived is not a form of superstition; rather, it is a reasonable means of strengthening religious commitment and as useful to naturalistic religion as to supernaturalistic religion.

Having considered the role of ritual in a naturalistic religion, let us next turn to the concept of prayer. It might be thought that naturalistic religion could have no use for prayer, since prayer is supposedly addressed to a supernatural being, and proponents of naturalistic religion do not believe in the existence of such a being. But this objection oversimplifies the concept of prayer, focusing attention on one type while neglecting an equally important but different sort.

Supernaturalistic religion makes extensive use of petitionary prayer, prayer that petitions a supernatural being for various favors. These may range all the way from the personal happiness of the petitioner to the general welfare of all society. Since petitionary prayer rests on the assumption that a supernatural being exists, such prayer clearly has no place in a naturalistic religion.

Not all prayers, however, are prayers of petition. Some prayers are prayers of meditation. These are not directed to any supernatural being and are not requests for the granting of favors. Rather, these prayers provide the opportunity for persons to rethink their ultimate commitments and rededicate themselves to live up to their ideals. Such prayers may take the form of silent devotion or may involve oral repetition of certain central texts. Just as Americans repeat the Pledge of Allegiance and reread the Gettysburg Address, so adherents of naturalistic religion repeat the statements of their ideals and reread the documents that embody their traditional beliefs.

It is true that supernaturalistic religions, to the extent that they utilize prayers of meditation, tend to treat these prayers irrationally, by supposing that if the prayers are not uttered a precise number of times under certain specified conditions, then the prayers lose all value. Yet prayer need not be viewed in this way. Rather, as the British biologist Julian Huxley wrote, prayer "permits the bringing before the mind of a world of thought which in most people must inevitably be absent during the occupations of ordinary life: . . . it is the means by which the mind may fix itself upon this or that noble or beautiful or awe-inspiring idea, and so grow to it and come to realize it more fully".[2]

Such a use of prayer may be enhanced by song, instrumental music, and various types of symbolism. These elements, fused together, provide the means for adherents of naturalistic religion to engage in religious services akin to those engaged in by adherents of supernaturalistic religion. The difference between the two services is that those who attend the latter come to relate themselves to God, while those who attend the former come to relate themselves to their fellow human beings and to the world in which we live.

We have so far discussed how ritual and prayer can be utilized in naturalistic religion, but to adopt a religious perspective also involves metaphysical beliefs and moral commitments. Can these be maintained without recourse to supernaturalism?

If we use the term "metaphysics" in its usual sense, referring to the systematic study of the most basic features of existence, then a metaphysical system may be either supernaturalistic or naturalistic. The views of Plato, Descartes, and Leibniz are representative of a supernaturalistic theory; the views of Aristotle, Spinoza, and Dewey are representative of a naturalistic theory.

Spinoza's *Ethics,* for example, one of the greatest metaphysical works ever written, explicitly rejects the view that any being exists apart from Nature itself. Spinoza identifies God with Nature as a whole and urges that the good life consists in coming to understand Nature. In his words, "our salvation, or blessedness, or freedom consists in a constant and eternal love toward God."[3] Spinoza's concept of God, however, is explicitly not the supernaturalistic concept of God, and Spinoza's metaphysical system thus exemplifies not only a naturalistic metaphysics but also the possibility of reinterpreting the concept of God within a naturalistic framework.

Can those who do not believe in a supernaturalistic God commit themselves to moral principles, or is the acceptance of moral principles dependent on acceptance of supernaturalism? Some have assumed that those who reject a supernaturalistic God are necessarily immoral, for their denial of the existence of such a God leaves them free to act without fear of Divine punishment. This assumption, however, is seriously in error.

The refutation of the view that morality must rest upon belief in a supernatural God was provided more than two thousand years ago by Socrates in Plato's *Euthyphro.* Socrates asked the following question: Are actions right because God says they are right, or does God say actions are right because they are right? This question is not a verbal trick; on the contrary, it poses a serious dilemma for those who believe in a supernatural deity. Socrates was inquiring whether actions are right due to God's fiat or whether God is Himself subject to moral standards. If actions are right due to God's command, then anything God commands is right, even if He should command torture or murder. If one accepts this view, then it makes no sense to say that God Himself is good, for since the good is whatever God commands, to say that God commands rightly is simply to say that He commands as He commands, which is a tautology. This approach makes a mockery of morality, for might does not make right, even if the might is the infinite might of God. To act morally is not to act out of fear of punishment; it is not to act as one is commanded to act. Rather, it is to act as one ought to act. How one ought to act is not dependent on anyone's power, even if the power be Divine.

Thus actions are not right because God commands them; on the contrary, God commands them because they are right. What is right is independent of what God commands, for what He commands must conform with an independent standard in order to be right. Since one could act in accordance with this independent standard without believing in the existence of a supernatural God, it follows that morality does not rest upon supernaturalism. Consequently, naturalists can be highly moral (as well as immoral) persons, and supernaturalists can be highly immoral (as well as moral) persons. This conclusion should come as no surprise to anyone who has contrasted the life of Buddha, an atheist, with the life of the monk Torquemada, organizer of the Spanish Inquisition.

We have now seen that naturalistic religion is a genuine possibility, since reasonable individuals may perform rituals, utter prayers, accept metaphysical beliefs, and commit themselves to moral principles without believing in supernaturalism. Indeed, one can even do so while maintaining allegiance to Christianity or Judaism. Consider, for example, those Christians who accept the "Death of God"[4] or those Jews who adhere to Reconstructionist Judaism.[5]

Such options are philosophically respectable. Whether to choose any of them is for each reader to decide.

NOTES

1. Jack Cohen, *The Case for Religious Naturalism* (New York: Reconstructionist Press, 1958), p. 150.

2. Julian Huxley, *Religion Without Revelation* (New York: New American Library, 1957), p. 141.

3. Spinoza, *Ethics,* ed. James Gutmann (New York: Hafner, 1957), pt. 5, prop. 36, note.

4. See John H. T. Robinson, *Honest to God* (Philadelphia: Westminster, 1963).

5. See Mordecai M. Kaplan, *Judaism as a Civilization* (New York: Schocken, 1967).

III

MORALITY, SOCIETY, AND ART

11

A SUPREME MORAL PRINCIPLE?

Many thinkers have sought one basic principle that could serve as the ultimate ethical guide, requiring us to perform all the actions we ought to perform and forbidding us from performing all the actions we ought not perform. Which are the leading candidates for such a moral touchstone?

One common to various religious traditions is the Golden Rule. Its positive formulation, attributed to Jesus, is: "whatever you wish that men would do to you, do so to them."[1] The negative formulation, which appeared five hundred years earlier, is attributed to Confucius and was later proposed by the Jewish sage Hillel. The latter put it as follows: "What is hateful to you, do not to your neighbor."[2] Is either of these the supreme moral principle?

Consider first the positive formulation. Granted, we usually ought to treat others as we would wish them to treat us. For instance, we ought to go to the aid of an injured person, just as we would wish that person to come to our aid if we were injured. But if we always followed this rule, the results would be unfortunate. Consider masochists, who derive pleasure from being hurt. Were they to act according to the principle in question, their duty would be to inflict pain, thereby doing to others as they wish done to themselves. Similarly, consider a person who enjoys receiving telephone calls, regardless of who is calling. The principle would require the individual to telephone everyone, thereby reciprocating preferred treatment. Indeed, strictly speaking, it would be impossible to fulfill the positive formulation of the Golden Rule, for we wish so many others to do so much for us, we would not have time to do all that is necessary to treat them likewise. Indeed, as the philosopher Walter Kaufmann noted,

65

"anyone who tried to live up to Jesus' rule would become an insufferable nuisance."[3]

In this respect the negative formulation of the Golden Rule is preferable, for it does not imply that we have innumerable duties toward everyone else. Neither does it imply that masochists ought to inflict pain on others, nor that those who enjoy receiving telephone calls ought themselves to make calls. However, while the negative formulation does not require these actions, neither does it forbid them. It enjoins us not to do to others what is hateful to ourselves, but pain is not hateful to the masochist and calls are not hateful to the telephone enthusiast. Thus the negative formulation of the Golden Rule, although superior in a sense to the positive formulation, is not the supreme moral principle, since it does not prohibit actions that ought to be prohibited.

Let us next consider two other standards of conduct, each of which has sometimes been thought to be the supreme moral principle. One was originally formulated by Kant, who argued that the moral worth of an action is to be judged not by its consequences but by the nature of the maxim (the principle) that motivates the action. Thus, right actions are not necessarily those with favorable consequences but those performed in accordance with correct maxims. But which maxims are correct? According to Kant, only those that can serve as universal laws, since they are applicable to every person at any time without exception. In other words, you should act only on a maxim that can be universalized without contradiction.

To see what Kant had in mind, consider a specific example he used to illustrate his view. Suppose you need to borrow money, but it will be lent to you only if you promise to pay it back. You realize, however, that you will not be able to honor the debt. Is it permissible for you to promise to repay the money, knowing you will not keep that promise? Kant proposed that the way to determine whether such an action is permissible is to universalize the maxim in question and see whether it leads to contradiction. The maxim is: Whenever I am short of money, I shall borrow it, promising to pay it back even if I know I shall not do so. Can this maxim be universalized without contradiction? Kant argued that it cannot.

> For supposing it to be a universal law that everyone when he thinks himself in a difficulty should be able to promise whatever he pleases, with the purpose of not keeping his promise, the promise itself would become impossible, as well as the end that one might have in view in it, since no one would consider that anything was promised to him, but would ridicule all such statements as vain pretenses.[4]

In other words, to make promises with no intention of keeping them would lead to the destruction of the practice of promising. Thus since the maxim in question cannot be universalized without contradiction, it is not morally acceptable and, consequently, any action it motivates is immoral. According to Kant, then, the supreme moral principle is: *"Act only on that maxim whereby thou canst at the same time will that it should become a universal law."*[5]

Unfortunately, this principle prohibits actions that ought to be permitted. Although we might agree that the maxim of making insincere promises cannot be universalized, we can easily imagine cases in which a person ought to make a promise without any intention of keeping it. Suppose, for example, you and your family will starve to death unless you obtain food immediately, and a very wealthy person offers to provide the food if you will promise repayment within twenty-four hours. Surely we would say, contrary to Kant's principle, under these circumstances you ought to act on a maxim that cannot be universalized and make a promise you have no intention of keeping.

Kant's insistence that proper maxims admit of no exceptions leads him not only to approve morally repugnant actions but also to sanction some that are inconsistent. Maxims he approves may conflict, and in that case adherence to one involves the violation of another. In the preceding case, for instance, were you to act in accord with the maxim of never making insincere promises, you would violate another maxim affirmed by Kant, that of aiding those who are in distress. He argues that both maxims admit of no exceptions, but since always to abide by both is impossible, Kant's position appears to lead to contradiction.

Perhaps his proposal fails because it concentrates exclusively on the reason for an action and fails to take into account its results. So let us next consider a principle that focuses on consequences, one defended by Mill. He was a leading advocate for the ethical position known as utilitarianism, according to which an action is right insofar as it promotes the happiness of mankind and wrong insofar as it promotes unhappiness. By the term "happiness" Mill means pleasure and the absence of pain. By the term "mankind" he means all persons, each valued equally. So Mill's supreme moral principle is: Act in such a way as to produce the greatest pleasure for the greatest number of people, each person's pleasure counting equally.

This principle avoids the pitfalls of Kant's view, for whereas he admitted no exceptions to moral rules and was thus led to condemn insincere promises that saved human lives, the utilitarian principle is flexible enough to allow for any exceptions that increase overall happiness. Although Mill would agree that insincere promises are usually wrong, since they are apt to cause more pain than pleasure, he would allow that in some cases, such as that of the starving family, an insincere promise is morally justifiable, for it would lead to greater overall happiness than any alternative.

The flexibility of the utilitarian principle is an advantage but also a fatal flaw, for it permits action that ought to be prohibited. Consider, for example, inhabitants of a city who each week abduct a stranger and place the unfortunate person in an arena to wrestle a lion. When the inhabitants of the city are challenged to justify this practice, they reply that although one person suffers much pain, thousands of spectators obtain greater pleasure from this form of entertainment than from any other, and so the spectacle is justified on utilitarian grounds. Clearly Mill's principle here yields an unacceptable implication. And other cases along similar lines likewise illustrate the laxity of utilitarianism. The sheriff who hangs an innocent person to satisfy the vengeance of the townspeople may maximize pleasure but nevertheless acts irresponsibly.

One way to try to salvage the utilitarian principle is to argue that not all pleasures are of equal quality, that, for example, the pleasure of spectators at a lion arena is less valuable than that enjoyed by those at a piano recital. As Mill put it, "It is better to be a human being dissatisfied than a pig satisfied; better to be Socrates dissatisfied than a fool satisfied. And if the fool, or the pig, are a different opinion, it is because they only know their own side of the question. The other party to the comparison knows both sides."[6]

This move is dubious, for some individuals, knowing both sides of the question, would prefer to witness a struggle between human and lion rather than between human and keyboard. And even if only one knowledgeable individual had such taste, why should that person's view be disregarded? Furthermore, Mill's principle cannot be salvaged by the claim that attendance at a piano recital develops sensitivity whereas a visit to a lion arena dulls it, for, according to utilitarianism, actions are good to the extent that they produce pleasure, not the extent that they produce sensitivity.

Perhaps, given the complexities of the human condition, any search for a supreme moral principle is doomed to failure, but the analysis so far has at least succeeded in calling attention to one fundamental feature of morality. The positive and negative formulations of the Golden Rule, the Kantian principle, and utilitarianism all serve as reminders that a moral person is obligated to be sensitive to others. This insight motivates not only the biblical injunction to treat our fellow human beings as we wish to be treated, but also the utilitarian insistence that each person's happiness is to count neither more nor less than another's. The same theme is central to Kant's view, a point he made explicit by claiming that his supreme moral principle could be reformulated as follows: "So act as to treat humanity, whether in thine own person or in that of any other, in every case as an end and never as means only."[7]

The moral point of view thus involves taking into account interests apart from our own. Do we ever do so? According to the theory known as egoism, all human behavior is motivated only by self-interest. On this view all individuals act solely in an effort to increase their own pleasure; people are kind to others only if they believe that such kindness will eventually redound to their own benefit. Thus no person would ever be a moral agent, for no one would ever act from genuinely altruistic considerations. Is egoism correct?

On the surface the theory seems clearly mistaken. Consider, for instance, a doctor who is devoted to serving the poor and has no interest whatever in publicizing this work. Doesn't such a case refute egoism?

A defender of the theory is apt to reply that this doctor only appears to be acting altruistically but is, in fact, acting selfishly, deriving pleasure from ministering to others. The egoist claims that the doctor is as selfish as the rest of us, but whereas we enjoy owning cars and attending parties, the doctor enjoys living a simple life and providing medical aid to the poor. All of us seek to maximize our pleasure, but since we differ in what we enjoy, we act in different ways. Nevertheless, the underlying motive in every case is self-interest.

The egoistic line of argument is impervious to counterexamples, but this invulnerability reveals the theory as vacuous, a reflection not of empirical evidence but of an arbitrary decision to use words idiosyncratically. The egoist declares us selfish if we act to fulfill our own desires. How are those identified? According to the egoist, we desire to do whatever we actually do, even if we are sacrificing ourselves for others. But then to say that we act as we desire is to say merely that we act as we act, which is a tautology. If we are declared selfish simply because we act as we act, then, of course, we all act selfishly, but such a definition is obviously a misuse of the term "selfish." As James Rachels notes: "The mere fact that I am acting on *my* wants does not mean that I am acting selfishly; that depends on *what it is* that I want."[8] An unselfish person cares about the welfare of others, whereas a selfish person does not. The tautology that all of us act as we act does not obliterate the distinction between an unselfish and a selfish person, no matter how the meaning of words is distorted. Thus the egoist's challenge to morality fails.

While most of us sometimes act altruistically, why should we do so on those occasions when our self-interest dictates otherwise?

This final question rests on the assumption that we can sometimes be sure that acting immorally is to our own advantage. But, as Hume noted, "[K]naves, with all their pretended cunning and abilities, [are] betrayed by their own maxims; and while they purpose to cheat with moderation and secrecy, a tempting incident occurs, nature is frail, and they give in to the snare; whence they can never extricate themselves, without a total loss of reputation, and the forfeiture of all future trust and confidence with mankind."[9] In short, immorality invariably threatens self-interest, and rarely, if ever, can this menace be sufficiently minimized to render the risk worthwhile.

What if someone wishes to take the chance and is unmoved by altruistic considerations? Can we reason further? Perhaps in such a case we can only repeat the words of the French maximist La Rochefoucauld: "To virtue's credit we must confess that our greatest misfortunes are brought about by vice."[10] In sum, when sympathy is missing, morality rests on practicality.

NOTES

1. *The Holy Bible: Revised Standard Version* (New York: Thomas Nelson and Sons, 1952), Matthew 7:12.

2. *The Babylonian Talmud* (London: Soncino Press, 1938), Shabbath, 31a.

3. Walter Kaufmann, *The Faith of a Heretic* (New York: Doubleday, 1963), p. 212.

4. Immanuel Kant, *Foundations of the Metaphysics of Morals*, trans. Lewis White Beck (New York: Liberal Arts Press, 1959), p. 40.

5. *Ibid.*, p. 39.

6. John Stuart Mill, *Utilitarianism* (Indianapolis: Hackett, 1979), p. 10.

7. Kant, p. 47.

8. "Egoism and Moral Scepticism," in Steven M. Cahn, *A New Introduction to Philosophy* (New York: Harper & Row, 1971), p. 426.

9. David Hume, *An Enquiry Concerning the Principles of Morals* (Indianapolis: Hackett, 1983), p. 82.

10. *The Maxims of La Rochefoucauld*, trans. Louis Kronenberger (New York: Random House, 1959), #183.

12

TWO CONCEPTS OF AFFIRMATIVE ACTION

In March 1961, less than two months after assuming office, President John F. Kennedy issued Executive Order 10925, establishing the President's Committee on Equal Employment Opportunity. Its mission was to end discrimination in employment by the government and its contractors. The order required every federal contract to include the pledge that "The contractor will not discriminate against any employe[e] or applicant for employment because of race, creed, color, or national origin. The contractor will take affirmative action to ensure that applicants are employed, and that employe[e]s are treated during employment, without regard to their race, creed, color, or national origin."

Here, for the first time in the context of civil rights, the government called for "affirmative action." The term meant taking appropriate steps to eradicate the then widespread practices of racial, religious, and ethnic discrimination.[1] The goal, as the president stated, was "equal opportunity in employment."

In other words, *procedural* affirmative action, as I shall call it, was instituted to ensure that applicants for positions would be judged without any consideration of their race, religion, or national origin. These criteria were declared irrelevant. Taking them into account was forbidden.

The Civil Rights Act of 1964 restated and broadened the application of this principle. Title VI declared that "No person in the United States shall, on the ground of race, color or national origin, be excluded from participation in, be denied the benefits of, or be subjected to discrimination under any program or activity receiving Federal financial assistance."

But before one year had passed, President Lyndon B. Johnson argued that fairness required more than a commitment to such procedural affirmative

71

action. In his 1965 commencement address at Howard University, he said, "You do not take a person who for years has been hobbled by chains and liberate him, bring him up to the starting line of a race and then say, 'you're free to compete with all the others,' and still justly believe that you have been completely fair."

And so several months later Johnson issued Executive Order 11246, stating that "It is the policy of the Government of the United States to provide equal opportunity in Federal employment for all qualified persons, to prohibit discrimination in employment because of race, creed, color or national origin, and to promote the full realization of equal employment opportunity through a positive, continuing program in each department and agency." Two years later the order was amended to prohibit discrimination on the basis of sex.

While the aim of Johnson's order is stated in language similar to that of Kennedy's, Johnson's abolished the Committee on Equal Employment Opportunity, transferred its responsibilities to the Secretary of Labor, and authorized the secretary to "adopt such rules and regulations and issue such orders as he deems necessary and appropriate to achieve the purposes thereof."

Acting on this mandate, the Department of Labor in December 1971, during the administration of President Richard M. Nixon, issued Revised Order No. 4, requiring all federal contractors to develop "an acceptable affirmative action program," including "an analysis of areas within which the contractor is deficient in the utilization of minority groups and women, and further, goals and timetables to which the contractor's good faith efforts must be directed to correct the deficiencies." Contractors were instructed to take the term "minority groups" to refer to "Negroes, American Indians, Orientals, and Spanish Surnamed Americans." (No guidance was given as to whether having only one parent, grandparent, or great-grandparent from a group would suffice to establish group membership.) The concept of "underutilization," according to the Revised Order, meant "having fewer minorities or women in a particular job classification than would reasonably be expected by their availability." "Goals" were not to be "rigid and inflexible quotas," but "targets reasonably attainable by means of applying every good faith effort to make all aspects of the entire affirmative action program work."[2]

Such *preferential* affirmative action, as I shall call it, requires that attention be paid to the same criteria of race, sex, and ethnicity that procedural affirmative action deems irrelevant. Is such use of these criteria justifiable in employment decisions?[3]

Return to President Johnson's claim that a person hobbled by discrimination cannot in fairness be expected to be competitive. How is it to be determined which specific individuals are entitled to a compensatory advantage? To decide each case on its own merits would be possible, but this approach would undermine the argument for instituting preferential affirmative action on a group basis. For if some members of a group are able to compete, why not others? Thus defenders of preferential affirmative action maintain that the group, not the individual, is to be judged. If the group has suffered discrimination, then all its members are to be treated as hobbled runners.

But note that while a hobbled runner, provided with a sufficient lead in a race, may cross the finish line first, giving that person an edge prevents the individual from being considered as fast a runner as others. An equally fast runner does not need an advantage to be competitive.

This entire racing analogy thus encourages stereotypical thinking. For example, recall those men who played in baseball's Negro Leagues. That these athletes were barred from competing in the Major Leagues is the greatest stain on the history of the sport. But while they suffered discrimination, they were as proficient as their counterparts in the Major Leagues. They needed only to be judged by the same criteria as all others, and ensuring such equality of consideration is the essence of procedural affirmative action.

Granted, if individuals are unprepared or ill-equipped to compete, then they ought to be helped to try to achieve their goals. But such aid is appropriate for all who need it, not merely for members of particular racial, sexual, or ethnic groups.

Victims of discrimination deserve compensation. Former players in the Negro Leagues ought to receive special consideration in the arrangement of pension plans and any other benefits formerly denied them due to unfair treatment. The case for such compensation, however, does not imply that present Black players vying for jobs in the Major Leagues should be evaluated in any other way than their performance on the field. To assume their inability to compete is derogatory and erroneous.

Such considerations have led recent defenders of preferential affirmative action to rely less heavily on any argument that implies the attribution of noncompetitiveness to an entire population.[4] Instead the emphasis has been placed on recognizing the benefits society is said to derive from encouraging expression of the varied experiences, outlooks, and values of members of different groups.

This approach makes a virtue of what has come to be called "diversity."[5] As a defense of preferential affirmative action, it has at least two advantages. First, those previously excluded are now included not as a favor to them but as a means of enriching all. Second, no one is viewed as hobbled; each competes on a par, although with varied strengths.

Note that diversity requires preferential hiring. Those who enhance diversity are to be preferred to those who do not. But those preferred are not being chosen because of their deficiency; the larger group is deficient lacking diversity. By including those who embody it, the group is enhanced.

But what does it mean to say that a group lacks diversity? Or to put the question another way, would it be possible to decide which member of a ten-person group to eliminate in order to decrease most markedly its diversity?

So stated, the question is reminiscent of a provocative puzzle in *The Tyranny of Testing*, a 1962 book by the scientist Banesh Hoffman. In this attack on the importance placed on multiple-choice tests, he quotes the following letter to the editor of the *Times* of London:

> Sir.—Among the "odd one out" type of questions which my son had to answer for a school entrance examination was: "Which is the odd one out among cricket, football, billiards, and hockey?" [In England "football" refers to the game Americans call "soccer," and "hockey" here refers to "field hockey."]

The letter continued:

> I said billiards because it is the only one played indoors. A colleague says football because it is the only one in which the ball is not struck by an implement. A neighbour says cricket because in all the other games the object is to put the ball into a net. . . . Could any of your readers put me out of my misery by stating what is the correct answer . . . ?

A day later the *Times* printed the following two letters:

> Sir.—"Billiards" is the obvious answer . . . because it is the only one of the games listed which is not a team game.

> Sir.— . . . football is the odd one out because . . . it is played with an inflated ball as compared with the solid ball used in each of the other three.

Hoffman then continued his own discussion:

> When I had read these three letters it seemed to me that good cases had been made for football and billiards, and that the case for cricket was par-

ticularly clever. . . . At first I thought this made hockey easily the worst of the four choices and, in effect, ruled it out. But then I realized that the very fact that hockey was the only one that could be thus ruled out gave it so striking a quality of separateness as to make it an excellent answer after all—perhaps the best.

Fortunately, for my peace of mind, it soon occurred to me that hockey is the only one of the four games that is played with a curved implement.

The following day the *Times* published yet another letter, this from a philosophically sophicated thinker.

> Sir.—[The author of the original letter] . . . has put his finger on what has long been a matter of great amusement to me. Of the four—cricket, football, billiards, hockey—each is unique in a multitude of respects. For example, billiards is the only one in which the colour of the balls matters, the only one played with more than one ball at once, the only one played on a green cloth and not on a field. . . .
>
> It seems to me that those who have been responsible for inventing this kind of brain teaser have been ignorant of the elementary philosophical fact that every thing is at once unique and a member of a wider class.

With this sound principle in mind, return to the problem of deciding which member of a ten-person group to eliminate in order to decrease most markedly its diversity. Unless the sort of diversity is specified, the question has no rational answer.

In searches for college and university faculty members, we know what sorts of diversity are typically of present concern: race, sex, and certain ethnicities. Why should these characteristics be given special consideration?

Consider, for example, other nonacademic respects in which prospective faculty appointees can differ: age, religion, nationality, regional background, economic class, social stratum, military experience, bodily appearance, physical soundness, sexual orientation, marital status, ethical standards, political commitments, and cultural values. Why should we not seek diversity of these sorts?

To some extent schools do. Many colleges and universities indicate in advertisements for faculty positions that they seek persons with disabilities or Vietnam War veterans. The City University of New York requires all searches to give preference to individuals of Italian-American descent.

The crucial point is that the appeal to diversity never favors any particular candidate. Each one adds to some sort of diversity but not another. In a department of ten, one individual might be the only black, another the only woman, another the only bachelor, another the only veteran, another the only one over 50, another the only Catholic, another the only Republican, another the only Scandinavian, another the only socialist, and the tenth the only Southerner.

Suppose the suggestion is made that the sorts of diversity to be sought are those of groups that have suffered discrimination. This approach leads to another problem, clearly put by the philosopher John Kekes:

> It is true that American blacks, Native Americans, Hispanics, and women have suffered injustice as a group. But so have homosexuals, epileptics, the urban and the rural poor, the physically ugly, those whose careers were ruined by McCarthyism, prostitutes, the obese, and so forth. . . .
>
> There have been some attempts to deny that there is an analogy between these two classes of victims. It has been said that the first were unjustly discriminated against due to racial or sexual prejudice and that this is not true of the second. This is indeed so. But why should we accept the suggestion . . . that the only form of injustice relevant to preferential treatment is that which is due to racial or sexual prejudice? Injustice occurs in many forms, and those who value justice will surely object to all of them.[6]

Kekes's reasoning is cogent. But another difficulty looms for the proposal to seek diversity only of groups that have suffered discrimination. For diversity is supposed to be valued not as compensation to the disadvantaged, but as a means of enriching all.

Consider, for example, a department in which most of the faculty members are women. In certain fields such as nursing and elementary education, such departments are common. If diversity by sex is of value, then such a department, when making its next appointment, should prefer a man. But men as a group have not been victims of discrimination. So to achieve valued sorts of diversity, the question is not which groups have been discriminated against, but which valued groups are not represented. The question thus reappears as to which sorts of diversity are to be most highly valued. I know of no compelling answer.

Seeking to justify preferential affirmative action in terms of its contribution to diversity raises yet another difficulty. For preferential affirmative action is commonly defended as a temporary rather than a permanent measure.[7] Yet preferential affirmative action to achieve diversity is not temporary.

Suppose it were. Then once an institution had appointed an appropriate number of members of a particular group, preferential affirmative action would no longer be in effect. Yet the institution may later find that it has too few members of that group. Since lack of valuable diversity is presumably no more acceptable at one time than another, preferential affirmative action would have to be reinstituted. Thereby it would in effect become a permanent policy.

Why do so many of its defenders wish it to be only transitional? They believe the policy was instituted in response to irrelevant criteria for appointment having been mistakenly treated as relevant. To adopt any policy that continues to treat essentially irrelevant criteria as relevant is to share the guilt of those who discriminated originally. Irrelevant criteria should be recognized as such and abandoned as soon as feasible.

Some defenders of preferential affirmative action argue, however, that an individual's race, sex, or ethnicity is germane to fulfilling the responsibilities of a faculty member. They believe, therefore, that preferential affirmative action should be a permanent feature of search processes, since it takes account of criteria that should be considered in every appointment.

At least three reasons have been offered to justify the claim that those of a particular race, sex, or ethnicity are particularly well-suited to be faculty members. First, it has been argued that they would be especially effective teachers of any student who shares their race, sex, or ethnicity.[8] Second, they have been supposed to be particularly insightful researchers due to their experiencing the world from distinctive standpoints.[9] Third, they have been taken to be role models, demonstrating that those of a particular race, sex, or ethnicity can perform effectively as faculty members.[10]

Consider each of these claims in turn. As to the presumed teaching effectiveness of the individuals in question, no empirical study supports the claim.[11] But assume compelling evidence were presented. It would have no implications for individual cases. A particular person who does not share race, sex, or ethnicity with students might teach them superbly. An individual of the students' own race, sex, or ethnicity might be ineffective. Regardless of statistical correlations, what is crucial is that individuals be able to teach effectively all sorts of students, and it is entirely consistent with procedural affirmative action to seek individuals who give evidence of satisfying this criterion. But knowing an individual's race, sex, or ethnicity does not reveal whether that person will be effective in the classroom.

Do members of a particular race, sex, or ethnicity share a distinctive intellectual perspective that enhances their scholarship? The philosopher Celia Wolf-Devine has aptly described this claim as a form of "stereotyping" that is "demeaning." As she puts it, "A Hispanic who is a Republican is no less a Hispanic, and a woman who is not a feminist is no less a woman."[12] Furthermore, are Hispanic men and women supposed to have the same point of view in virtue of their common ethnicity, or are they supposed to have different points of view in virtue of their different sexes?

If our standpoints are thought to be determined by our race, sex, and ethnicity, why not also by the numerous other significant respects in which people differ, such as age, religion, sexual orientation, and so on? Since each of us is unique, can anyone else share my point of view?

That my own experience is my own is a tautology that does not imply the keenness of my insight into my experience. The victim of a crime may as a result embrace an outlandish theory of racism. But neither who you are nor what you experience guarantees the truth of your theories.

To be an effective researcher calls for discernment, imagination, and perseverance. These attributes are not tied to one's race, sex, ethnicity, age, or religion. Black scholars, for example, may be more inclined to study Black literature than are non-Black scholars. But some non-Black literary critics are more interested in and more knowledgeable about Black literature than are some Black literary critics. Why make decisions based on fallible racial generalizations when judgments of individual merit are obtainable and more reliable?

Perhaps the answer lies in the claim that only those of a particular race, sex, or ethnicity can serve as role models, exemplifying to members of a particular group the possibility of their success. Again, no empirical study supports the claim, but in this case it has often been taken as self-evident that, for instance, only a woman can be a role model for a woman, only a Black for a Black, only a Catholic for a Catholic. In other words, the crucial feature of a person is supposed to be not what the person does but who the person *is*.

The logic of the situation, however, is not so clear. Consider, for example, a Black man who is a Catholic. Presumably he serves as a role model for Blacks, men, and Catholics. Does he serve as a role model for Black women, or can only a Black woman serve that purpose? Does he serve as a role model for all Catholics or only for those who are Black? Can I serve as a role model for anyone else, since no one else shares all my characteristics? Or perhaps I can serve as a role model for everyone else, since everyone else belongs to at least one group to which I belong.

Putting aside these conundrums, the critical point is supposed to be that in a field in which discrimination has been rife, a successful individual who belongs to the discriminated group demonstrates that members of the group can succeed in that field. Obviously success is possible without a role model, for the first successful individual had none. But suppose persuasive evidence were offered that a role model, while not necessary, sometimes is helpful, not only to those who belong to the group in question, but also to those prone to believe that no members of the group can perform effectively within the field. Role models would then both encourage members of a group that had suffered discrimination and discourage further discrimination against the group.

To serve these purposes, however, the person chosen would need to be viewed as having been selected by the same criteria as all others. If not, members of the group that has suffered discrimination as well as those prone to discriminate would be confirmed in their common view that members of the group never would have been chosen unless membership in the group had been taken into account. Those who suffered discrimination would conclude that it still exists, while those prone to discriminate would conclude that members of the group lack the necessary attributes to compete equally.

How can we ensure that a person chosen for a position has been selected by the same criteria as all others? Preferential affirmative action fails to serve the purpose, since by definition it differentiates among people on the basis of criteria other than performance. The approach that ensures merit selection is procedural affirmative action. By its demand for vigilance against every form of discrimination, it maximizes equal opportunity for all.

The policy of appointing others than the best qualified has not produced a harmonious society in which prejudice is transcended and all enjoy the benefits of self-esteem. Rather, the practice has bred doubts about the abilities of those chosen while generating resentment in those passed over.

Procedural affirmative action had barely begun before it was replaced by preferential affirmative action. The difficulties with the latter are now clear. Before deeming them necessary evils in the struggle to overcome pervasive prejudice, why not try scrupulous enforcement of procedural affirmative action? We might thereby most directly achieve that equitable society so ardently desired by every person of good will.

NOTES

1. A comprehensive history of one well-documented case of such discrimination is Dan A. Oren, *Joining the Club: A History of Jews and Yale* (New Haven: Yale University Press, 1985). Prior to the end of World War II, no Jew had ever been appointed to the rank of full professor in Yale College.

2. 41 C.F.R. 60–2.12. The Order provides no suggestion as to whether a "good faith effort" implies only showing preference among equally qualified candidates (the "tie-breaking" model), preferring a strong candidate to an even stronger one (the "plus factor" model), preferring a merely qualified candidate to

a strongly qualified candidate (the "trumping" model), or canceling a search unless a qualified candidate of the preferred sort is available (the "quota" model).

A significant source of misunderstanding about affirmative action results from both the government's failure to clarify which type of preference is called for by a "good faith effort" and the failure on the part of those conducting searches to inform applicants which type of preference is in use. Regarding the latter issue, see my "Colleges Should be Explicit About Who Will Be Considered for Jobs," *The Chronicle of Higher Education, XXXV* (30), 1989, reprinted in *Affirmative Action and the University: A Philosophical Inquiry*, Steven M. Cahn (ed.), (Philadelphia: Temple University Press, 1993), pp. 3–4 (chapter 14 in this book).

3. Whether their use is appropriate in a school's admission and scholarship decisions is a different issue, involving other considerations, and I shall not explore that subject in this essay.

4. See, for example, Leslie Pickering Francis, "In Defense of Affirmative Action," in Cahn, *op. cit.*, especially pp. 24–26. She raises concerns about unfairness to those individuals forced by circumstances not of their own making to bear all the costs of compensation, as well as injustices to those who have been equally victimized but are not members of specified groups.

5. The term gained currency when Justice Lewis Powell, in his pivotal opinion in the Supreme Court's 1979 *Bakke* decision, found "the attainment of a diverse student body" to be a goal that might justify the use of race in student admissions. An incisive analysis of that decision is Carl Cohen, *Naked Racial Preference* (Lanham, Md.: Madison Books, 1995), pp. 55–80.

6. Cahn, *op. cit.*, p. 151.

7. Consider Michael Rosenfeld, *Affirmative Action and Justice: A Philosophical and Constitutional Inquiry* (New Haven: Yale University Press, 1991), p. 336: "Ironically, the sooner affirmative action is allowed to complete its mission, the sooner the need for it will altogether disappear."

8. See, for example, Francis, *op. cit.*, p. 31.

9. See, for example, Richard Wassersstrom, "The University and the Case for Preferential Treatment," *American Philosophical Quarterly, 13* (4), 1976, pp. 165–170.

10. See, for example, Joel J. Kupperman, "Affirmative Action: Relevant Knowledge and Relevant Ignorance," in Cahn, *op. cit.*, pp. 181–188.

11. Consider Judith Jarvis Thomson, "Preferential Hiring," *Philosophy and Public Affairs, 2* (4), 1973, p. 368: "I do not think that as a student I learned any better, or any more, from the women who taught me than from the men, and I do not think that my own women students now learn any better or any more from me than they do from my male colleagues."

12. Cahn, *op. cit.*, p. 230.

13

THE CURIOUS TALE OF
ATLAS COLLEGE

Atlas College, a liberal arts institution, was founded during the middle of the nineteenth century. At that time the Board of Trustees adopted as the school's motto the maxim of the Roman poet Juvenal, *mens sana in corpore sano*, "a sound mind in a sound body." The saying attracted little notice over the years, but several decades ago a recently appointed member of the board complained at a Trustees' meeting that, while attending a reception to greet members of the faculty, he had found to his dismay that the school's professors were not physically well-conditioned, most appearing either scrawny or corpulent. "How," he inquired of his fellow Board members, "can these individuals exemplify the ideals of our College, if they fail to display soundness of body?"

Thus he urged the Board to adopt as school policy the principle that henceforth all persons appointed to faculty positions should be of normal weight, understood as no more than ten percent above or below desirable weights for men and women as listed in an authoritative medical textbook. The members of the Board, following the encouragement of its long-time leader, a former captain of the Atlas football team, agreed to institute the idea, not as a written rule but as an informal guideline to be conveyed by the president to all administrators and members of search committees.

From that time on, all applicants for faculty positions were required to fill out weight forms. Individuals outside the weight limits were dropped from further consideration. They were never told officially they had been eliminated because of weight, but the policy became widely known. If an applicant appeared for an interview and was suspected of having falsified the weight form, the person was asked to step on a scale in the Dean's office and, if excessively overweight or underweight, eliminated from the search.

The faculty gradually included more and more individuals of normal weight. Those professors who held tenure at the time the new policy was instituted were not affected, but as they retired or left, they were replaced by those who met the new guidelines.

Eventually this practice came to the attention of the Equal Employment Opportunity Commission in Washington, D.C., which ordered Atlas to cease discriminating against applicants for faculty positions on the basis of weight. Officials at Atlas agreed to comply. But, in fact, no one other than those of normal weight was ever appointed.

When this situation was recognized by the Commission, a dispute arose among its members as to the proper remedy. One side urged that Atlas be monitored carefully to insure that its processes were free of weight discrimination. Such a procedure would have required that administrators at Atlas be prepared to explain each of their appointments and respond fully to any questions posed by investigators from the Commission. If the responses had shown evidence of bad faith, Atlas would have been taken to court, and, assuming the judge agreed with the Commission, Atlas would have been forced by legal order to cease its discriminatory practices or face severe fines.

Others on the Commission, however, believed that this approach would be excessively time-consuming and susceptible to evasive action by wily administrators at Atlas, who might appoint at most one or two token overweight and underweight individuals while continuing a policy of discrimination. These Commission members called for the implementation of a plan that, in accord with the language and intent of federal guidelines, would require Atlas to develop "goals and timetables" that would specify the steps Atlas would take so as no longer to be "deficient" in its "utilization" of overweight or underweight individuals.

The Commission members who favored this latter plan won the day. Therefore Atlas was forced to commit itself to specific employment targets. As a result, the school began to increase the number of those it now referred to as the "differently sized." The College's newly created Office of Appointment Processes regularly reported to the Commission, and the Office was especially pleased one particular year to announce that its goal had been exceeded, that more differently sized people had been appointed than had been targeted.

Why did the plan work so well? The Office had developed special procedures to insure that goals were attained. All applicants were asked to fill out weight forms. Those differently sized were identified, and their progress was monitored throughout the search process. When applicants appeared for interviews, they were asked to step on a scale in the Office of Appointment Processes to confirm that their weight forms had been filled out accurately. If no qualified applicants for a position fulfilled the weight guidelines, then the search was canceled.

Eventually the number of differently sized faculty members at Atlas reached the national average, and the issue arose as to whether the Office of Appointment Processes should continue to keep track of the relevant statistics. The director of the Office argued for the need to do so, insisting that otherwise the number of differently sized faculty members might decrease, and in that case the College would be in danger of being found again in violation of federal guidelines, especially in view of Atlas's poor past record. So the administration decided that it would be prudent to go on monitoring the situation and continue to encourage departments to recruit the differently sized.

To aid in this effort, applicants for positions at Atlas still fill out weight forms and are weighed during campus interviews. Should any candidate object to those procedures, that person is reminded of the history of discrimination at Atlas and the need to guard against any relapse.

The Board member who had originally raised this issue has now retired. But he is not entirely displeased with the outcome. Admittedly, the presence on the faculty of any overweight or underweight individuals is contrary to his wish, but he has been vindicated in his belief that a person's weight should be relevant to an academic appointment. After all, applicants for faculty positions continue to fill out weight forms, and the most promising candidates are weighed. Thus weight matters at the College, as he thought it should.

Justice has thus run its course at Atlas. Or has it?

14

WHY NOT TELL THE TRUTH?

A fundamental principle of academic ethics is that the announcement of any available faculty or administrative position should make clear whatever special criteria the institution has established for choosing among applicants. Criteria not specified should not be used.

Today virtually every college or university advertising a position in the *Chronicle of Higher Education* describes itself as an "Equal Opportunity/ Affirmative Action Employer," sometimes adding that it "welcomes and encourages applications from women and minority candidates" (and occasionally "Vietnam-era veterans" or "persons with disabilities"). While such phrases are always supposed to signify that the college or university does not engage in discrimination, sometimes the same words are also intended to convey the important message that the institution strongly prefers, or will give serious consideration only to, members of specific groups.

In fairness to all applicants, shouldn't departments and schools be explicit about such matters? If it has been agreed internally that membership in particular groups is to be given strong weight in the decision procedure, shouldn't the announcement of the position say so? And in instances in which an institution has decided to fill a position only if a qualified member of a particular group or groups can be found, shouldn't this information, too, be stated candidly?

Several university presidents recently announced that they had committed their institutions to appointing (within a fixed time) a specific number of faculty members from certain groups. At one university the administration's policy is to make available a faculty position for any department that finds a qualified Black candidate. At another university the board of trustees has created five new faculty positions designated specifically for

85

Black scholars. Search committees at those institutions are instructed to make choices that will help achieve the stated objectives. Shouldn't job announcements from those schools inform potential applicants of the special situations, so that people who are, and people who are not, members of the groups in question can decide whether to apply for the positions in light of full information about the conditions governing the searches?

Not everyone agrees about the most effective and equitable actions colleges can take to remedy injustice. But whatever the criteria in effect for an appointment, the faculty members and administrators who established them surely considered them to be within ethical and legal bounds.

Why not state these criteria publicly, without ambiguity or deception? Why not tell the truth?

15

THE DIVESTITURE PUZZLE

I

Suppose I hold one hundred shares of stock in a company that has embarked on a policy I consider immoral. I, therefore, wish to divest myself of those one hundred shares. For me to sell them, someone must buy them. But the buyer would be purchasing one hundred shares of "tainted" stock, and I would have abetted the buyer in this immoral course of action. Granted, the prospective buyer might not believe the stock "tainted," but that consideration would be irrelevant to me, since I am convinced that, knowingly or unknowingly, the buyer would be doing what is immoral. Surely I should not take any steps that would assist or encourage the buyer in such deplorable conduct. Nor should I try to release myself from a moral predicament by entangling someone else. How then is principled divestiture possible?

II

This puzzle does not purport to prove that divestiture is invariably a mistake but only that it cannot ever be justified as a moral imperative. Yet three attempts to solve the problem, those by Daniel H. Cohen,[1] Kerry S. Walters,[2] and David Gordon and James Sadowsky[3] all seek to demonstrate how divestiture might be defended on grounds other than that of moral principle, a point not in dispute.

Walters agrees that by divesting one becomes "a reluctant accessory in . . . an immoral situation." Yet he defends divestiture as a second-best

87

but still acceptable alternative for those more concerned with their own peace of mind than that of others.

Principled divestiture, however, is divestiture based on principle. The action is supposed to flow from moral duty. So the issue is not, as Walters would have it, whether divestiture is permitted but whether it is required. And he admits that, far from being morally requisite, divestiture is not even "fully virtuous," since it results in "slightly soiled hands." So he has highlighted the problem but not solved it.

Cohen takes a different tack from Walters, responding that I have misunderstood the purpose of divestiture. It is not intended "to cleanse individuals' portfolios and souls," a "self-righteous" goal, but to force the stock's price down and thereby bring external pressure on the company to change its policy.

But the question is not whether divestiture can be defended on strategic grounds. Surely it can be. Likewise, it can be opposed on strategic grounds, for by not divesting a stockholder maintains the leverage to bring internal pressure on the company to change its policy. Either strategy may succeed or fail, depending in any particular case on a variety of factors, including the percentage of total outstanding shares held, the attitudes of the board of directors, social and economic conditions, and so on.

The puzzle I presented focused not on such empirical considerations but on the axiom that, regardless of circumstances, the only ethically proper policy is to sell "tainted" stock. So Gordon and Sadowsky's conclusion that under the given conditions "one cannot avoid acting badly" and must, therefore, make a decision based solely on "consequentialist grounds" supports my position.

As for the suggestion they attribute to D. R. Steele that a possessor of "tainted" stock might choose to renounce ownership rather than sell, this financially fatal strategy would amount to redistribution of the value of the divestor's shares among all other stockholders. The assets of those who had not divested would thereby be increased as would presumably their moral culpability.

The question thus remains as I put it previously: how is principled divestiture possible?

III

In attempting to dissolve this puzzle, Roger A. Shiner[4] argues that since the seller does not cause the buyer to act, does not "force, coerce, entice, or otherwise influence" the buyer, but merely "occasions a situation in which someone does wrong," the seller maintains moral integrity. As Shiner says, "Whoever will own my shares will indeed do wrong. But that is not my problem."

Selling, however, does not merely occasion buying; one person's selling *is* another's buying. "A sells X to B" and "B buys X from A" are not two events but one. Seeking to disentangle them is futile.

So is the attempt to avoid moral responsibility for one's desires. Your wish to sell your stock is logically equivalent to your wishing someone to buy it. But, by hypothesis, you believe it wrong for anyone to buy it. So your wish to sell is the wish that someone else do wrong. And that desire is immoral.

The divestiture puzzle thus remains unsolved.

NOTES

1. *Analysis* 48.2, pp. 175–176.
2. *Analysis* 48.4, pp. 216–218.
3. *Analysis* 49.3, pp. 153–155.
4. *Analysis* 50.3, pp. 205–210.

16

THE STRANGE CASE OF
JOHN SHMARB

I

(with L. Michael Griffel)

One morning Art Freund opened his newspaper and was astonished to come upon the following headline: "FIND MANUSCRIPT OF BRAHMS'S FIFTH SYMPHONY: LOST WORK UNCOVERED IN VIENNA HOME." The accompanying story reported that a grandson of a former student of Brahms, rummaging through an old family trunk, had unearthed some dusty pages that turned out to be an original Brahms manuscript: a fifth symphony completed just prior to the composer's death in 1897. It had never been performed or published, and, in fact, Brahms seems never to have even mentioned it to anyone. According to the newspaper, members of the illustrious Vienna music circle, having seen the score, enthusiastically agreed that the work was a worthy companion to its four famous predecessors.

But they were no more enthusiastic than Art, who firmly resolved to attend the premier of the Fifth Symphony in Vienna on May 7, the anniversary of Brahms' birth. Only with great difficulty did Art manage to obtain a ticket, for all the most celebrated members of the music world were to be in attendance on this momentous occasion.

When that great day finally arrived, Art's expectations were fully realized. The music was magnificent and the audience response overwhelming.

Critics spoke with impassioned, unqualified admiration for the new masterpiece. The *Times* reported:

> The four extended movements of the Symphony are each of the highest order and exemplify many of the composer's finest traits. The intense agitation and propulsion of the opening allegro appassionata, the lilting Viennese charm of the andante, the scherzo's cross-rhythms and explosive climaxes, the all'ongarese melodies of the theme and variations finale all testify to the strong Brahmsian character of the piece. But the special significance of the composition is its unusual tendencies toward a cyclical structure, most apparent in the use of the first-movement theme to link the end of the scherzo with the finale. In addition, the main theme of the second movement returns as a counterpoint to the final variation of the last movement. Interestingly, the work is marked by the use of many more non-functional harmonic progressions than one encounters in Brahms's other symphonies. This feature gives the work a forward-moving restlessness and enormous impact.

A story later in the week announced that the first recording of the Fifth Symphony would be released at the end of the year by the Berlin Philharmonia. When Art arrived home, he found in his mailbox publicity releases from leading American orchestras advising subscribers that performances of the new masterpiece would be scheduled immediately upon publication of the eagerly awaited score, already in progress.

Several weeks later Art was shocked by another headline: "BRAHMS'S FIFTH SYMPHONY A FAKE: MUSIC WORLD AGHAST." Incredibly, the symphony had actually been the handiwork of a young American composer, John Shmarb, who had called a press conference to announce his achievement. He explained that after managing to obtain authentic paper and ink of the nineteenth century, he had forged Brahms's handwriting and arranged to have the manuscript found in the old trunk. When asked why he had concocted such an elaborate hoax, young Shmarb replied:

> For the last ten years, publishers and critics and musicologists have been dismissing my work as inconsequential because they claimed all I did was copy nineteenth-century music. Well, I finally got fed up. They weren't being fair to my music. Now that the world has judged my work as it would judge the work of any nineteenth-century composer, my genius has been acknowledged. I am not imitating Brahms. I am simply composing as a contemporary of Brahms might have. I find it natural to write in the Romantic vein and want to continue to do so. A great work is a great work, whether composed by Brahms or by Shmarb.

Response to Shmarb's words was swift and unanimously harsh. One German critic typified the attitude of many by denouncing Shmarb as an unscrupulous fraud. "The outrage of it all! Having us waste our time on such worthless music is criminal. Shmarb has shown himself to be a musical charlatan." A leading American avant-garde composer commented: "Shmarb has always been incapable of utilizing his natural abilities. His output is merely derivative. Another sad case of misdirected and misused talent." Word soon followed that the Berlin Philharmonia had eliminated the symphony from its recording schedule, that plans to publish the work had been abandoned at considerable cost to the publisher, and that all announced performances had been canceled.

Art was greatly disheartened at these disclosures, for his cherished experience of attending the premiere of a major Brahms work had been turned into participation in a hoax. But the more he thought about the situation, the more upset he became, for he gradually realized that an even greater disappointment was that he would never again hear that symphony he had so much enjoyed. Shmarb's words ran through his mind: "A great work is a great work." He wondered why the same critics who had praised the symphony earlier now condemned it as worthless. For, he thought, did the great Brahms symphony suddenly become a poor work just because it was written by Shmarb in 1968? Suppose it had been written by Stravinsky in 1928 or by Bruckner in 1888? Would it be a finer composition or more enjoyable? Is it impossible to judge the merit of an anonymous composition because the composer and date are unknown? Why cannot a composer be permitted to choose for himself the style in which he wishes to compose, whether that style is original in its time, typical of its time, or typical of an earlier time? Stylistic originality has been the gift of only a few composers in the history of music. Most works, indeed most of the outstanding and best-loved musical compositions, have been written in an established idiom. Stylistic originality can be a virtue, but it is not a necessity in the creation of great art. Inventiveness within a style, though more common than radical stylistic originality, is nevertheless deserving of equal consideration. Inventiveness within a particular style is possible for any composer writing at any time within that style.

After all, certain styles, such as that of the late Romantic period, are beloved by audiences around the world. Why must they hear only old works, composed centuries ago, in those styles? Why can they not hear compositions written by contemporary composers in classic styles that have endured the test of time?

The more Art pondered the matter, the more disturbed he was by the public response to Shmarb's symphony. He very much wanted to hear the work again and have the opportunity to confirm his judgment that it was a masterpiece. Surely, he thought, listening to the music itself is the only sensible way to evaluate it. What other way could possibly be appropriate?

II

Apart from its musical structure, what do we know of Shmarb's Symphony? Only that critics and audiences admired it greatly and, because of factors in part external to the music, thought it a composition by Brahms. Yet, although never having heard the work, Gordon Epperson[1] disparages it as "imitative" and "derivative," while Neil Courtney[2] calls its admirers "sycophants" and assures us it "would never survive extended exposure to true music lovers."

Both these commentators appear certain that great composers display such individuality that no piece by one could be thought to have been written by anyone else. This claim has historically been proven false. Debates have raged for decades over the authenticity of various musical, artistic, and literary works sometimes attributed to one of the masters. Might we not hear a section of the incomparable Mozart C-Minor Piano Concerto and suppose it written by Beethoven? Haven't sophisticated listeners sometimes confused a scene by Rossini with one by Donizetti? Indeed, all "true music lovers" have had the experience of turning on the radio in the middle of a lovely selection and mistaking its composer.

So if Shmarb's Symphony was thought to have been written by Brahms, why is the piece necessarily inferior? Before making a judgment, I would want to hear the music. To do otherwise, as Epperson eventually puts it, would be an aesthetic "injustice."

NOTES

1. "The Strange Case of John Shmarb: Some Further Thoughts," *Journal of Aesthetics and Art Criticism* XXXIV, 1, 1975, pp. 23–25.

2. "The Strange Case of John Shmarb: An Epilogue and Further Reflections," *Journal of Aesthetics and Art Criticism* XXXIV, 1, 1975, pp. 27–28.

17

THE WIFE OF LEAR

The dramatis personae for that summit of tragic literature, *King Lear*, includes Lear, King of Britain, and his three daughters—but not his wife. Do we ever learn anything about her, or does she remain a cipher?

The sole direct reference to her occurs in Act II, scene iv, when Lear, speaking to Regan, refers to "thy mother's tomb." So Lear's wife, the Queen of Britain and the "lawful" (IV, vi) mother of Goneril, Regan and Cordelia, had died.

Have we any clue to the sort of person she was? We do if make the ordinary assumption that the personality of children reflects the personality of at least one of their parents. Such is the case with Cordelia and Lear. Both are proud, stubborn, and capable of fidelity and love. Indeed, their very likeness leads them into conflict at the beginning of the play and into reconciliation at the end.

But Goneril and Regan have nothing in common with their father. These daughters are capable of treachery and cruelty that lie beyond his comprehension. Who was the model for their malevolence? The obvious answer is: their mother.

How did Cordelia escape her mother's baneful influence? Remember that as the play opens Cordelia is quite young, not yet married, while the wife of Lear, no longer discussed, has presumably been dead many years. So of all three daughters Cordelia knew her mother for the shortest time, perhaps hardly at all. Unlike her sisters, Cordelia was raised under the primary guidance not of her mother but of her father. Thus their affinity.

But by what means could an iniquitous woman have persuaded Lear to make her his Queen? We can almost hear her beguiling him with the same deceits later mimicked by her perfidious daughters:

> Sir, I love you more than word can wield the matter;
> Dearer than eyesight, space, and liberty;
> Beyond what can be valued, rich or rare;
> No less than life, with grace, health, beauty, honor; (I, i)

We are all prone to repeat our mistakes. So was Lear. The evidence suggests that at the terrible moment he was led toward his own destruction by the false flattery of Goneril and Regan, their hypocritical words echoed those uttered on another occasion many years before, when the powerful yet gullible King had been duped by the wiles of another woman.

IV

EDUCATION

18

JOHN DEWEY AT EIGHTY

In late 1939 John Dewey reached his eightieth birthday, an anniversary that occasioned tributes in newspapers and periodicals throughout the country. The American Philosophical Association named Dewey its honorary president and requested that he retain this title for the duration of his life. Also timed to coincide with the celebration was the publication of the initial volume of Paul Arthur Schlipp's *The Library of Living Philosophers*. This book provided a critical analysis and evaluation of Dewey's philosophy by such contemporaries as Bertrand Russell, George Santayana, Hans Reichenbach, and Alfred North Whitehead. Schilpp's choice of Dewey as the first honoree is clearly justified by one of Whitehead's remarks in the volume: "We are living in the midst of the period subject to Dewey's influence."[1] Whitehead went on to stress the significance of Dewey's philosophical thought for the development of American civilization, and he classed Dewey with philosophers whom he viewed as having performed an analogous role in their own societies—Augustine, Aquinas, Descartes, and Locke.

Most remarkably, while his friends and admirers were planning ways of honoring him for a lifetime of achievements, Dewey not only continued to publish articles at an extraordinary rate but also produced three longer works that are among his finest writings: *Theory of Valuation, Experience and Education,* and *Freedom and Culture.*[2] Such an accomplishment at so advanced an age is astonishing and, I believe, unparalleled in the history of philosophy.

Dewey's philosophical interests were wide-ranging, including metaphysics, epistemology and philosophy of science, ethics, social and political philosophy, aesthetics, and philosophy of education. In our own day, when many admired philosophers rarely venture outside their chosen specialties, it is well to remember that most members of the philosophical pantheon assumed that their systems of thought had explanatory power in all fields of philosophical inquiry, and they did not hesitate to test the adequacy of their principal ideas by applying them in one field after another. Dewey followed this tradition and thereby made significant contributions to virtually every area of philosophy.

He consistently maintained that the most reliable method of reaching the truth about any subject matter is the pattern of inquiry exemplified in science: the evaluation of hypotheses by drawing their implications and subjecting them to empirical testing under controlled conditions. In short, Dewey stressed that ideas are to be judged not by their origins but by their consequences.

The most common objection to his view comes from those who grant the scientific method's effectiveness in acquiring factual knowledge but question its usefulness in determining matters of value. Dewey explicitly replied to this familiar challenge in his *Theory of Valuation,* a monograph he contributed to *The Foundations of the Unity of Science,* a two-volume work edited by Otto Neurath, an Austrian philosopher who was a leading member of the Vienna Circle, that group of logical positivists centered in Vienna University during the 1920s and 1930s.

As is evident from the monograph, Dewey had his differences with the logical positivists, but he liked Neurath personally and was persuaded by him to contribute to the project. The charming story of how Neurath succeeded in enlisting Dewey's participation was told by Ernest Nagel:

> I accompanied Neurath and Sidney Hook when they called on Dewey at his home; and Neurath was having obvious difficulty in obtaining Dewey's participation in the *Encyclopedia* venture. Dewey had one objection—there may have been others, but this is the one I recall—to Neurath's invitation. The objection was that since the Logical Positivists subscribed to the belief in atomic facts or atomic propositions, and since Dewey did not think there are such things, he could not readily contribute to the *Encyclopedia.*
>
> Now at that time Neurath spoke only broken English, and his attempts at explaining his version of Logical Positivism were not very successful. Those of us who knew Neurath will remember his elephantine sort of physique. When he realized that his efforts at explanation were getting him nowhere, he got up, raised his right hand as if he were taking an oath in a court of law (thereby almost filling Dewey's living room), and solemnly declared, "I *swear* we don't believe in atomic propositions." This pronouncement won the day for Neurath. Dewey agreed

to write the monograph, and ended by saying, "Well, we ought to cele-brate," and brought out the liquor and mixed a drink.[3]

Thus did Dewey come to write *Theory of Valuation.*

The essence of his view about the nature of ethical judgments is that they are neither mere expressions of emotion nor revelations of a transcendent order but rather statements of human ideals, emerging from and testable in experience. What is desired, therefore, may not prove desirable, once consideration is given both to the means needed to achieve the ends and the consequences of the ends themselves.

Dewey's stress on the continuity of means and ends has led some critics to suppose that he denied the concept of an end-in-itself. Brand Blanshard, for example, asked, "What is it that has led Dewey to this strange theory that we can attach no value to ends in themselves?"[4] Dewey, however, proposed no such theory. As he wrote in *Democracy and Education*: "All that we can be sure of educationally is that science should be taught so as to be an end in itself in the lives of students—something worthwhile on account of its own unique intrinsic contribution to the experience of life."[5] And he continued on to make the general point: "Some goods are not good *for* anything; they are just goods. Any other notion leads to an absurdity. For we cannot stop asking the question about an instrumental good, one whose value lies in its being good *for* something, unless there is at some point something intrinsically good, good for itself."[6]

Dewey stressed, however, that intelligent choices need to be made among goods and that doing so depends on empirical considerations. "For example, an end suggests itself. But, when things are weighed as means toward that end, it is found that it will take too much time or too great an expenditure of energy to achieve it, or that, if it were attained, it would bring with it certain accompanying inconveniences and the promise of future troubles. It is then appraised and rejected as a 'bad' end."[7] In this way the experimental method can inform valuation.

Just as Dewey's ethical theory steered between the Scylla and Charybdis of emotivism and intuitionism, so his educational theory also avoided two hazardous alternatives. Already in 1902 in *The Child and the Curriculum,* Dewey had identified the weaknesses in what he then termed "old education" and "new education."

Proponents of the former view considered the curriculum to be the keystone of the educational process. As Dewey stated their position, "Subject-mater furnishes the end, and it determines method. The child is simply the immature being who is to be matured; he is the superficial being who is to be deepened; his is the narrow experience which is to be widened. It is his to receive, to accept. His part is fulfilled when he is ductile and docile."[8] The emphasis here is on order and discipline; the teacher is supposed to command, the student to obey.

On the other hand proponents of "new education" disregarded the curriculum and focused attention exclusively on the child. Dewey characterized their outlook as follows: "Literally, we must take our stand with the child and our departure from him. It is he and not the subject-matter which determines both quality and quantity of learning. . . . The source of whatever is dead, mechanical, and formal in schools is found precisely in the subordination of the life and experience of the child to the curriculum."[9] The emphasis here is on spontaneity and freedom. And if the student is to display initiative, the teacher must not interfere in the learning process.

In short, "old education" subordinated the child to the curriculum; "new education" subordinated the curriculum to the child. "Old education" required the teacher to be active and the student to be passive. "New education" required the student to be active and the teacher to be passive.

Perhaps the most pervasive misunderstanding in twentieth-century educational thought is the supposition that Dewey advocated "new education." In fact, he was as opposed to "new education" as to "old education." Here is Dewey commenting on "new education":

> The child is expected to "develop" this or that fact or truth out of his own mind. He is told to think things out, or work things out for himself, without being supplied any of the environing conditions which are requisite to start and guide thought. Nothing can be developed from nothing; nothing but the crude can be developed out of the crude—and this is what surely happens when we throw the child back upon his achieved self as a finality, and invite him to spin new truths of nature or of conduct out of that.[10]

But what precisely did Dewey propose in place of both "old education" and "new education"? In his view the teacher's responsibility is to direct the learning process so that the child's immature powers find fulfillment in that systematized outcome of human inquiry we call "the curriculum." The aim of instruction is to discover a path from the child's own experience to the maturity of human experience reflected in art, science, and industry. A teacher who disregards the child and focuses exclusively on the curriculum is like a tour guide who reaches the proper destination but has left the party far behind. A teacher who disregards the curriculum and focuses exclusively on the child is akin to the guide who remains with the party but does not lead them anywhere. Dewey insisted that we cannot afford to neglect either the child or the curriculum; sacrificing one for the other amounts to educational failure.

Proponents of "old education" and "new education" continued their battle throughout the early decades of the twentieth century. All that changed were the labels by which their respective positions were known. In 1938, when Dewey published *Experience and Education,* a series of lectures delivered to the honorary society Kappa Delta Pi, he no longer referred to "old education" and "new education" but instead spoke of "traditional education" and "progressive education."

The latter term requires special comment, since Dewey is himself so often identified as the leading proponent of progressive education. In fact, however, "progressive education" was a term he rarely used. He preferred to talk of education for a "progressive society," by which he simply meant a society that progresses, that improves from generation to generation. Dewey viewed progressive education as nothing more or less than an education that imbues individuals with intelligence, the power of scientific method, and thus enables their society to better itself, to progress.

The term "progressive education" became a shibboleth used by those who in Dewey's name argued for a position identical with that previously called "new education," a position, as we have seen, Dewey opposed. In *Experience and Education* Dewey explicitly states his opposition to progressive education, misunderstood as the rejection of pedagogical authority and the glorification of student caprice. It cannot be overemphasized that Dewey never fell into the trap of supposing that to recognize the dignity of each student requires the teacher to abandon the role of leader of group activities. Indeed, Dewey quoted with admiration Ralph Waldo Emerson's dictum: "Respect the child, respect him to the end, but also respect yourself." [11]

Dewey made clear that the teacher is properly held responsible for what is going on in the classroom, and with responsibility goes authority. To recognize such authority, however, is not to suggest that the teacher should act in an authoritarian manner, exercising complete control over the will of students. The appropriate relationship is that of guide, not god. *Experience and Education* analyzes and illustrates the appropriate scope and limits of this guiding role.

While educational controversies of the late 1930s were remarkably similar to disputes about schooling that had occurred three decades before, the social, political, and economic situation in the United States on the eve of World War II was hardly like that of the early 1900s and was soon to be subject to unprecedented changes occurring at an ever-accelerating rate. How remarkable, therefore, that when Dewey at the age of eighty published *Freedom and Culture,* a study of the elements of culture that contribute to the maintenance of political freedom, he did not merely propose old solutions to new problems but provided a prophetic analysis of conditions, both internal and external, that in the years to come would seriously threaten the welfare of our democracy.

He emphasized, for instance, that the racial and religious prejudice prevalent in the United States during the 1930s corroded decency and undermined trust in human nature. At a time when discrimination against Catholics, Jews, and Blacks was the rule rather than the exception, Dewey recognized the evil inherent in such hatred and warned of its dangerous potential for crippling the democratic way of life.

He also recognized how similar were dictatorships of the right and the left. He noted that whether a government is Fascist or Communist, it inevitably suppresses basic freedoms, persecutes dissenters, and glorifies the Leader. While others at the time were sympathetic to the policies of the Russian government, Dewey opposed every form of totalitarianism, including the Soviet version, and he insisted on the importance of open discussion, voluntary associations, and free elections.

Nor did Dewey fall prey to isolationism. After the German offensives of 1939, he strongly supported American efforts to stem the Fascist tide. And he fully appreciated, as many of his contemporaries did not, the interlocking of national and international affairs. Even before the nuclear age, he wrote of how, due to remote influences, "we are at the mercy of events acting upon us in unexpected, abrupt, and violent ways."[12]

One of the central themes of *Freedom and Culture* is that individuals in the modern world increasingly find themselves in the grip of immense forces they can neither control nor understand. Dewey realized that new technologies were leading to the concentration of capital in enormous corporations, the interdependence of government and industry, and, perhaps most importantly, the enormous power of what we now refer to as "the media."

He provided an especially incisive description of this latter phenomenon, emphasizing how modern forms of communication can distract the public with trivia, sensationalize events and arouse confused emotions, promulgate partisan views under the guise of serving the public interest, and, in short, create what he termed "pseudo-public opinion."[13] Particularly noteworthy is Dewey's delineation of these problems years before the era of television.

What steps did he propose in the face of the weakening of the effects of individual action? He refused to subscribe to what he considered the oversimplified programs of Marxism or laissez-faire capitalism but, instead, urged unwavering commitment to democratic procedures of government, the enhancement of community life, and significant steps toward the equalization of those economic conditions he viewed as essential to equal rights.

Most importantly, Dewey believed that our control over events can be greatly enhanced by the spread of the scientific attitude in our schools and reliance on it in the resolution of public problems and the creation of cultural values. He emphasized that a democratic society is especially well-suited to promote the scientific method, for both democracy and science depend on "freedom of inquiry, toleration of diverse views, freedom of communication, the distribution of what is found out to every individual as the ultimate intellectual consumer."[14]

Dewey concluded *Freedom and Culture* not by proposing a specific political platform but by calling for "collective intelligence operating in cooperative action."[15] This characteristic phrase highlights the essence of his philosophical position: a commitment to a free society, critical intelligence, and the education required for their advance.

Dewey viewed philosophy of education as the most significant phase of philosophy. Charles Frankel once noted that for Dewey "all philosophy was at bottom social philosophy implicitly or explicitly."[16] I would extend this insight and suggest that for Dewey all social philosophy was at bottom philosophy of education implicitly or explicitly. As he put it, "it would be difficult to find a single important problem of general philosophic inquiry that does not come to a burning focus in matters of the determination of the proper subject matter of studies, the choice of methods of teaching, and the problem of the social organization and administration of the schools."[17]

Other philosophers, of course, have recognized the importance of education. Kant, for example, wrote that "the greatest and most difficult problem to which man can devote himself is the problem of education."[18] But I know of only two major philosophers who exemplified this principle in their philosophical work: one was Dewey, the other was Plato. He, too, found it difficult to discuss any important philosophical problem without reference to the appropriateness of various subjects of study, methods of teaching, or strategies of learning.

But while Dewey's philosophy of education rested on his belief in democracy and the power of scientific method, Plato's philosophy of education rested on his belief in aristocracy and the power of pure reason. Plato proposed a planned society, Dewey a society engaged in continuous planning. Plato considered dialectical speculation to be the means toward the attainment of truth; Dewey maintained that knowledge is only acquired through intelligent action. And whereas Plato divided the members of his ideal society into three classes, Dewey countered that what Plato had overlooked is that "each individual constitutes his own class."[19]

Suffice it to say that John Dewey is the only thinker ever to construct a philosophy of education comparable in scope and depth to that of Plato. And the three crucial works on which I have focused exhibit Dewey's thought in all its subtlety and power, reflecting eighty years of experience and a lifelong commitment to rendering all experience rational.

NOTES

1. *The Philosophy of John Dewey,* Library of Living Philosophers, ed. Paul Arthur Schlipp (New York: Tudor, 1951), p. 477.

2. *The Later Works of John Dewey, 1925–1953,* vol. 13, ed. Jo Ann Boydston (Carbondale: Southern Illinois University Press, 1988).

3. *Dialogue on John Dewey,* ed. Corliss Lamont (New York: Horizon Press, 1959), pp. 11–12.

4. Brand Blanshard, *Reason and Goodness* (London: George Allen and Unwin, 1961), p. 180.

5. *The Middle Works of John Dewey, 1899–1924,* ed. Jo Ann Boydston (Carbondale: Southern Illinois University Press, 1980), 9:249.

6. *Ibid.,* p. 250.

7. *Later Works,* p. 212.

8. *Middle Works,* 2:276.

9. *Ibid.,* pp. 276–277.

10. *Ibid.,* p. 282.

11. *Middle Works,* 9:57.

12. *Later Works,* p. 94.

13. *Ibid.,* p. 168.

14. *Ibid.,* p. 135.

15. *Ibid.,* p. 188.

16. *New Studies in the Philosophy of John Dewey,* ed. Steven M. Cahn (Hanover, N.H.: University Press of New England, 1977), p. 5.

17. *Later Works,* p. 260.

18. Immanuel Kant, *Education* (Ann Arbor: University of Michigan Press, 1960), p. 11.

19. *Middle Works,* 9:96.

19

ARE THE HUMANITIES USEFUL?

John Dewey's philosophy of education focused primarily on issues of elementary and secondary schooling. But his criticisms of traditional education, for subordinating the student to the subject matter, and progressive education, for subordinating the subject matter to the student, apply equally at the college level. In this chapter and the next, I consider two recent theories of higher education, opposed to each other, but both in my judgment unsuccessful for reasons Dewey provided decades ago.

In *Toward Freedom and Dignity: The Humanities and the Idea of Humanity*, O. B. Hardison contends that "the subordination of men to things" has made modern society ill and that the cure lies in "aesthetic education," an education that aims to liberate the imagination by stressing what Hardison alternatively refers to as "the humanities" or "humanism." He cites Kant, Schiller, Rousseau, Pestalozzi, Herbart, Montessori, Dewey, Holt, and especially A. S. Neill as having proposed varieties of aesthetic education, and he describes in detail a graduate class in which he put his own beliefs to work by acting as "the net in an intellectual tennis game." The class, he tells us, "had obvious affinities to a sensitivity group," and good teaching, he believes, has a "kinship to therapy." Grades are part of a "system of punishments," tests are unnecessary, and the appeal to standards is most often "a basis for intimidation."

I find Hardison's reasoning unconvincing. Of course, we ought to examine the aims of studying the arts, history, and philosophy, but far more is to be gained from these subjects than "an expanded self of the self." And nothing whatever qualifies a college professor to be a therapist. In following out his educational schemes, Hardison arranged for his class to be taught by a two-person team of students. He found the presentations "wretched" and filled with "blatant hypocrisy" and "grotesque parody." What did Hardison do? "I puffed my pipe. At the end of the session, I arose, clapped students A and B on the back, and expressed gratification on their fine performance." Clearly, something is seriously amiss with an educational theory that in the name of humanity countenances such instances of deceit.

Hardison's first major error, suggested in the subtitle of his book, is a failure to recognize that the humanities do not rest on a single, commonly accepted idea of humanity. Hardison says that the idea of humanity he has in mind "begins with the premise that the understanding of human concerns must be rooted not in things and abstractions but in the living, impermanent, and imperfect tissue of human experience." On the next page, however, he goes on to say: "I could cite numerous antecedents in Plato and his followers and in Christian and non-Christian theology." But neither Plato nor most theologians would agree that genuine understanding is to be achieved through a study of what is impermanent and imperfect. Surely Plato's view is exactly the opposite. The crucial point is that humanists such as Plato, Kant, and Dewey (or Mill, Bradley, and Sartre) have very different ideas about the nature of humanity and human experience. Thus to be seriously concerned with the humanities one need not adopt any particular metaphysical or epistemological position.

Hardison's second major error is his assumption that if the humanities are useful then they are not "self-justifying ends." This mistaken view leads him into several contradictions. For example, he says that "you do not read *Macbeth* to learn about the evils of ambition," but further on he claims that the aim of humanistic education is the "understanding of human values." He denies "that reading Chaucer makes one wiser," but one hundred pages later he tells us that humanistic education "is our best way . . . of insuring that those who will have to confront the future will possess the means and training to make wise decisions." If Hardison recognized that the humanities are both intrinsically and instrumentally valuable, then he could avoid these contradictions and, furthermore, would have no need to criticize liberal education on the grounds that it defends the usefulness of the humanities. Hardison is here overlooking Dewey's insight that a subject which is appreciated on its own account is, as a result, even more useful when it is employed instrumentally.

Hardison's third major error is that in stressing the importance of the humanities in enriching human imagination, he overlooks the equally important role of the humanities in developing intellectual sophistication. To think philosophically, for example, is not just a matter of expressing one's feelings. There are sound arguments and unsound ones, valid arguments and invalid ones, reasonable arguments and unreasonable ones. Teaching students philosophy involves teaching them to think critically, and individuals are not themselves the final arbiter of how well they think. Similarly, one does not teach students musicology just by playing pieces for them and awaiting their haphazard responses. The students need to learn, for instance, the structure of a fugue, the difference between tonality and atonality, and how a theme is treated in a set of variations. Granted, philosophy involves more than recognizing invalid arguments, and musicology involves more than knowing the difference between a symphony and a concerto, but without these essentials the rest is bluff and fluff.

Hardison wants the members of his model class to regard him as their intellectual equal, but if he is only the students' equal, why is he receiving a paycheck, while his students are charged tuition? Hardison recognizes that "if you are talking about something it is always desirable to know what you are talking about," but he overlooks the truism that students in general are not so knowledgeable as their teachers regarding the subject matter; if the students were as knowledgeable, they would not be students. To recognize this situation is not, as Hardison claims, to treat the student as "an inferior being" in "a master–slave relation," but only to recognize that the student knows less philosophy or musicology than the teacher. And what is inhumane about that judgment?

Despite my serious reservation about Hardison's book, I should like to conclude on one positive note. Hardison devotes an entire chapter to examining the course offerings of an English department at a major state university. He points out convincingly the incoherence of the curriculum. As he puts it, the catalogue resembles "an archeological site," indicating "an abdication of the responsibility of professionals to understand what they are professing." Such curricular confusion is all too common in our colleges, and I join Hardison in deploring it.

NOTE

1. *Toward Freedom and Dignity: The Humanities and the Idea of Humanity* (Baltimore: Johns Hopkins University Press, 1972).

20

SHOULD LIBERAL EDUCATION CHANGE?

The key to understanding Eva T. H. Brann's *Paradoxes of Education in a Republic*[1] lies in an early footnote in which she claims that St. John's College, the institution where she teaches, is the only school anywhere that offers "a full-scale, stable liberal arts program combined with readings in the Western textual tradition." Since so many liberal arts colleges have encouraged or required their students to read the masterpieces of Western literature and study the major political, economic, and philosophical influences that have shaped the character of Western civilization, why does Brann adopt such an exclusionary viewpoint?

The answer is revealed throughout the book. Quite simply, Brann treats the works of the classical and medieval ages as though they constituted scripture, approachable only with devotion and piety. She considers Montaigne, Bacon, Descartes, Locke, and the other makers of the modern mind to be heretics, for they insisted on testing authority by appeal to evidence. Their works are to be read, but only because they memorialized the tradition even while repudiating it. Thomas Jefferson is singled out for special criticism, for he sinned through "indomitable self-reliance of judgment." He dared to question the wisdom of Plato and the divinity of Jesus. He even went so far as to favor neologies, thus repudiating the sanctity of language.

Brann believes that contemporary thinkers can do no better than to imitate Renaissance scholars, who refurbished the traditional canon through scholarly servicing of texts. She does not consider us capable of any other novelty; the possibility for original thought vanished three centuries ago. Brann is thus committed to the view that just about the time Newton was born, human creativity was exhausted.

What is the appropriate curriculum for a liberal arts college today? According to Brann, students are to be taught receptivity to "the truth" as contained exclusively in "the collection of texts generally recognized as the founding books of Western learning." Is it permissible to read works that place the original texts in historical perspective? No, for these texts are meant to be self-explanatory. Is it permissible to read contemporary textbooks in science or mathematics? No, for while Euclid's *Elements* and Galileo's *Dialogues Concerning Two New Sciences* convey "the order of inquiry" and are thus "vehicles of reflection," textbooks follow "a scheme of presentation" and lack "textual authority." Is it permissible to read works in social studies? No, for they are too problematic for undergraduates. Is it permissible to read books from outside the Western tradition? No, for Eastern learning is intended to train the soul rather than inform the intellect.

In the face of such curricular rigidity, one might argue that since significant changes occur in the world, collegiate studies ought to take account of those changes. Brann's retort is that we do not live in a period of change; there is only the illusion of newness; time is not of the essence. In short, Parmenides was right after all.

It is hardly surprising that Brann is led into paradox trying to defend such a clearly contrary-to-fact position. She argues that liberal education is essentially non-utilitarian, a view that causes her perplexity as to why such education is of enormous use to citizens of a free society. She assumes that acquiring a liberal education requires adopting an attitude of reverence toward certain texts, thus creating a problem as to how such an attitude can be instilled in members of a democracy who are in her view impatient with authority. She insists, too, that rationality precludes a shared public opinion, but then she must wonder how theorizing is possible in a society that rests on consensus.

Brann's extended discussion of these issues obscures her failure to confront well-known objections to the educational plan she is defending. Consider, for example, Sidney Hook's Deweyian critique of the St. John's curriculum, as telling against Brann's book as it was originally against the extravagant claims made by St. John's founders:

> Great books by all means; but why not also great pictures and symphonies, great plays and cinemas, great social changes and mass movements, as well as the great Armageddons of our own time? We can learn at least as much from the heroic tragedy of Warsaw as from the last stand at Thermopylae. . . . Those who fulminate against the degeneration of modern education because some schools pay attention to the bridges, waterways, and sanitation systems of our large cities, together with other great feats of engineering, regard it as perfectly proper to study and glow about the marvels of Roman aqueducts, plumbing, and roads. . . . Absorption in study of

the greatness of the past which does not quicken our sense for greatness in the present is a preparation for a life of intellectual snobbery. . . . In education as in life we must learn to look to ourselves as ancestors, not merely descendants.[2]

Dewey himself had issued a similar warning: "[T]he mistake of making the records and remains of the past the main material of education is that it cuts the vital connection of present and past and tends to make the past a rival of the present and the present a more or less futile imitation of the past."[3]

Perhaps the most revealing paragraph in Brann's work is the one in which she makes this startling admission: "By the tradition I mean, further, the books of the West, ancient, medieval, and modern, omitting, however, the post-Biblical Jewish and the Arabic writings—a major lacuna—because of my ignorance and their present inaccessibility." Consider that Brann is obviously a most diligent scholar, one whose erudition is displayed in several quotations per page of text, innumerable references in almost every paragraph to major and minor figures in the history of Western thought, as well as nearly two hundred footnotes packed with extensive bibliographical information. How is it possible that such a thorough researcher was unable to obtain translations of, for example, the writings of Maimonides or Averroes, when these are to be found in virtually any university library?

Or are those works inaccessible in a deeper sense? Are they too discomfiting to be approached by one unwilling even to question the mystery of the Incarnation and the sacredness of Christian scripture?

In fact, such Jewish and Arabic works constitute overwhelming evidence that we are inheritors not of one tradition but of a multiplicity of conflicting traditions. To blindly accept all is to embrace contradiction. Our responsibility is to make intelligent choices, and to do so requires precisely that Jeffersonian "self-reliance of judgment" which Brann finds so unsettling.

Her plea is that we concentrate "on thinking things anew rather than on thinking new things." Let us be grateful that the Greeks did not adhere to such a retrogressive precept.

NOTES

1. *Paradoxes of Education in a Republic* (Chicago: University of Chicago Press, 1979).

2. Sidney Hook, *Education for Modern Man, Second Edition* (New York: Alfred A. Knopf, 1963), pp. 126, 133.

3. *The Middle Works of John Dewey, 1899–1924,* ed. Jo Ann Boydston (Carbondale: Southern Illinois University Press, 1980), 9:81.

21

HOW TO IMPROVE
YOUR TEACHING

Teaching, like scholarship, has its challenges. For knowing a subject is no guarantee of knowing how to convey it effectively. We professors are all prone to certain strategic mistakes, and here I want to focus on three of them.[1]

First is the error of overestimating our audience's background knowledge, reasoning skills, powers of concentration, and interest in the subject. Beginning teachers are especially susceptible to this pitfall, because they typically come fresh from graduate school, where fellow students are well educated, skilled at argument, and deeply committed to philosophy. They know who St. Anselm was, how he formulated the ontological argument, and why Kant thought it unacceptable. Most important, they care deeply about such matters. Woe be it to instructors who walk into class assuming freshmen students share such knowledge and concerns.

I recall early in my teaching career discussing with an introductory class John Hospers's article, "Free Will and Psychoanalysis," in which he refers to the "Oedipus complex." I assumed my students would understand this reference and did not explain it. I soon realized my mistake, for not only was the Oedipus complex unfamiliar to them, but they also had never heard of Oedipus.

In such circumstances we tend to blame our students. But no matter how bright or well prepared they may be, they invariably do not know as much as we hope. Nor are they as interested in all aspects of the subject as we wish. These conditions are a given in any pedagogical situation. The challenge of teaching is to inform the uninformed and motivate the unmotivated. For a teacher to complain about such matters is akin to a surgeon's complaining that the patients are all sick.

We should try to make our subjects as interesting and clear as they can be to as many of our students as possible. A good teacher directs instruction not only at the best student, or at the top ten percent of the class, or even at the majority; instead, a good teacher aims to interest and instruct everyone in the class. All students pay tuition, not just the A students. Granted, we shall not succeed with every student. But when more than one or two students complain they are lost, many others, whether they realize so, are also in need of help.

Those who overestimate the audience may eventually become discouraged and fall prey to a second strategic error: underestimating the audience. As various experiments in educational psychology have demonstrated, the less expected from students, the less they accomplish. Ease soon brings boredom; challenge breeds interest and excitement.

Instead of leading students beyond what is familiar to them, the underestimator chooses topics and readings that allow students to remain mired in their own immediate interests. Admittedly, students may at first not be interested in the appropriate subject matter, but the aim of teaching is to make apparent the connections between seemingly esoteric material and the students' own sphere of experience. The proper subject then becomes the students' personal concern. A teacher is a guide, and a guide is expected to lead you into unfamiliar territory, not just stroll along as you revisit familiar haunts.

The underestimator, unwilling to treat students as responsible agents, typically fails to maintain deadlines; all excuses are accepted. One of the most popular teachers I have ever known, a man whose classes are packed semester after semester, insists that all papers be handed in by the announced time. Except in the direst circumstances, he accepts no late papers. Students admire his stance, for he is treating them as mature persons who are expected to take responsibility for their actions. Business people have deadlines to meet; so do doctors and lawyers. So should students.

The underestimator also engages in the all too common practice of inflating grades. At many schools today students are distinctive not when they are on the dean's list, but when they are off it. Were we to judge the intellectual state of the union by the number of A's awarded college students, our nation miraculously would seem to have been turned into a society of scholars.

Students deserve an honest appraisal of the quality of their work. To give an A to a student who has done mediocre work is pure deception. And those who unjustly receive high grades are hardly apt to learn the meaning of excellence.

But if overestimating and underestimating students are to be avoided, how to find the middle ground? No simple reply is available, just as Aristotle found no easy answer to the question of where the virtuous mean lies between the two extremes. But at the end of Book II of the *Nicomachean Ethics,* he remarks that "we must watch the errors which have the greatest attraction for us personally. . . . We must then draw ourselves away in the opposite direction, for by pulling away from error we shall reach the middle."[2] So if you are inclined to overestimate, try underestimating. If you are inclined to underestimate, try overestimating. In both cases you are likely to achieve the sought-after mean.

A third strategic mistake is the failure to do justice to our intellectual opponents. Whenever a professor states opinions not shared by other reputable scholars, students ought to be so informed. They are entitled to know whether their teacher is expressing a consensus or only a majority or minority viewpoint. It is appropriate for an instructor to defend personal beliefs, but serious alternatives should not be neglected. A teacher should consider this question: if another qualified instructor were in my place, might that individual offer judgments that conflict with those I have presented? If the answer is yes, teachers should alert students, thereby increasing their understanding of the relevant issues.

For example, I believe that free will and determinism are incompatible, and when I teach this issue I argue for my own position. But I also emphasize that my view is, in fact, a minority opinion. And I do my best to explain as persuasively as possible the arguments that have been offered by those with whom I disagree.

To test your own fairness in presenting and examining ideas, imagine that your intellectual opponents were in the classroom. Would they agree that at least some of their arguments had been treated adequately? If not, you need to make greater efforts to be fair to the opposition.

Professors who are partisans usually display this failure in their manner of responding to questions. Instead of encouraging each student to think independently and raise challenges, they engage in intimidation and expect acquiescence. Their aim is not education but indoctrination. Such attempts to foster ideological zeal may be in order at a political rally, but they are entirely inappropriate in a classroom. Philosophy teachers are supposed to be guiding a critical inquiry, and an essential feature of this process is for all participants, including the faculty member, to be open-minded.

I have one final suggestion for pedagogical improvement. While we often seek our colleagues' advice about our scholarly endeavors, rarely do we ask their judgments about our teaching. I think it not only appropriate but also advisable for faculty members to share syllabi and examinations. Just as our colleagues can sometimes spot omissions or mistakes in our written arguments, so they can identify an unbalanced syllabus or an ambiguous examination question.

Most important, however, is for teachers to visit one another's classes. Professors typically allow as class visitors auditors, friends or relatives of students, and even faculty members from other departments. Why, then, should the doors be locked against those most qualified to understand what is gong on? What would we think of surgeons who permitted their operating procedures to be observed by anyone except other surgeons?

A colleague in the back of the room watching the proceedings with an experienced and understanding eye can provide invaluable advice that will better our performance. Athletes improve by being observed; so do musicians; why shouldn't teachers?

The observer should not participate in the class unless invited but afterward should discuss with the instructor all aspects of the proceedings: how a question was well put, how discussion may have gone off the track, whether the instructor was audible, whether writing on the blackboard was visible, how a difficult concept might have been presented more clearly, or how an idea explained in one context could have been applied in another. The aim, of course, is not to destroy an individual's distinctive teaching style but to enhance it.

Let me conclude with one simple suggestion. Invite into your class someone you regard as an excellent teacher and a sympathetic soul. Explain to this person that you are seeking frank suggestions about how to improve your teaching. The experience will almost surely be revelatory.

NOTES

1. This paper was delivered during the 1987 Eastern Division Meetings of the American Philosophical Association at a panel arranged by the Committee on the Teaching of Philosophy.

2. *Nicomachean Ethics,* trans. Martin Ostwald (Indianapolis: Bobbs-Merrill, 1962), 1109b.

22

HOW TO TEACH
INTRODUCTORY PHILOSOPHY

Instructors usually structure introductory philosophy courses in one of four ways. The first uses readings grouped by topic and drawn from historical and contemporary sources. Students thereby become acquainted with major problems of philosophy, read important historical and contemporary writings on each subject, and are encouraged to think through issues for themselves. Historical philosophers are given a word but not the last word; contemporary philosophers are seen as innovators but not creators *ex nihilo*.

This approach, however, has its pitfalls. As students shift quickly from Aristotle to Locke to Rawls, they are tempted to treat these authors as contemporaries. Students can also lose hold of the threads that are supposed to connect the selections. Furthermore, excerpts taken out of context can be difficult to understand. Most important, the approach may do a disservice to major historical figures, since reading a few pages from a philosophical classic is somewhat akin to listening to a few measures from a great symphony—the overall effect is typically disappointing.

An alternative curriculum consists of studying several major historical works in their totality. An immediate advantage is that most students are more easily motivated to read a classic by a renowned thinker rather than an article by a recent scholar unfamiliar to them. In addition, most great works of the past, unlike contemporary journal articles, were not intended only for specialists. These masterpieces embody a breadth of vision that has inspired generations, and reading these works in their entirety is intellectually satisfying.

This approach, however, also has its disadvantages. It suggests that philosophy is mainly the contemplation of works written long ago. Students may be led to suppose that their sole obligation is to grasp what

119

others have said, not to think critically. This problem is magnified by the need to spend much time and effort struggling with unfamiliar terminology and trying to understand the concerns that motivated our intellectual forebearers. Philosophy can thus be turned into a passive tour of the past rather than an active inquiry of present importance. One further difficulty is that in jumping from one classic to another a student hurdles centuries and is in danger of losing historical perspective. On the reading list Hobbes's *Leviathan* may follow Plato's *Republic,* but in history two millennia intervened, and students unacquainted with what occurred during that period, even if only in philosophical thought, are apt to have a distorted view of how these works relate. An additional concern is that the fewer works read in such a course, the greater is the danger of student boredom. An instructor may delight in spending fifteen weeks studying Descartes' *Meditations,* but for the uninitiated the experience may become excruciating.

A third format offers a systematic study of the history of philosophy. Such a course emphasizes historical perspective, and students are apt to be excited by the array of great books and ideas. But beginners may not appreciate that philosophy is an ongoing enterprise and that its practitioners do not primarily pore over ancient texts but read contemporary journals and analyze contemporary issues. Philosophy, after all, is not just the history of philosophy.

A fourth format uses a single-authored textbook written with a student audience in mind. The obvious difficulty, however, is that, unlike physics or chemistry, philosophy does not consist of a body of accepted truths, and one author can hardly do justice to all competing viewpoints. Why should students be reading a textbook when they could be reading original materials? Granted, philosophy may be difficult to understand, and a textbook can ease the strain, but philosophical disagreement is best grasped by confronting various authors who have diverse styles and opinions, not by reading homogenized textbooks. And one designed to avoid giving the impression of uniformity is apt to confuse students, leading them to wonder why the author appears indecisive.

In the face of these difficulties inherent in any introductory course, how should a teacher proceed? The key is to be aware of the pitfalls inherent in whichever approach is chosen.

If instructors prefer a problem-oriented format, they should recognize the need to supply historical perspective and links between articles. Students can be reminded that the great philosophers wrote books, not five-page fragments, and can also be told something about the books from which the selections are chosen.

If instructors prefer a classics format, they should recognize the need to make clear that philosophical inquiry did not cease centuries ago, that philosophers continue to work on issues that concerned Leibniz or Hume, that we read these authors not to venerate them but to help ourselves think more clearly about issues facing us today. Students also need to be reminded that the authors chosen lived at different historical times and were influenced by them.

If instructors prefer a historical format, students should be encouraged to approach the material with a critical attitude. And they need to be alerted to contemporary discussions of traditional issues as found in recent books and journals.

If instructors choose a single-authored textbook, students ought to be reminded of the availability of perspectives other than that provided by one author. And an attempt should be made to stress the importance of historical writings in helping us think about today's problems.

Whichever format is chosen, a teacher should explain the available options and indicate the reasons behind a curricular decision. Students will then be less likely to identify philosophy with one particular approach. And this insight itself will provide increased understanding of the complex subject to which they are being introduced.

23

SEARCHING FOR ADMINISTRATORS: THE MISSING STEP

Every year numerous colleges and universities conduct elaborate searches for academic administrators, including all manner of deans, vice presidents, and provosts. In each case, the steps are remarkably similar. A search committee is formed, an advertisement is placed, a hundred or so applications are received, the list is shortened, letters of reference are obtained, another cut is made, campus interviews are conducted, recommendations are presented, and the final decision is announced.

The process is invariably exhausting, but the results are often disappointing. The candidate who appeared confident and genial during interviews may turn out in office to be ineffective, evasive, or irresponsible. The rejected candidate whose crusty manner or candid opinions put off some committee members may be offered an administrative position elsewhere and become widely admired for trustworthiness, conscientiousness, and acumen.

Some mistakes are, of course, inevitable. But at least judgments should be made on the basis of the best available evidence. At present, however, committees frequently deliberate in the dark. They proceed as if the most important information were to be found in a curriculum vitae, letters from a candidate's supporters, and observations of a candidate's demeanor in a series of brief meetings.

But the most reliable indicator of future performance is past performance. And the quality of past performance is not found in a vita, a supporter's letter, or a brief question-and-answer session. The vita lists the positions held, not the quality of performance in each position. An interview tells more about the candidate's surface personality and verbal facility than sagacity or dependability. As for letters of recommendation, they are notoriously unhelpful. Even Stalin could have obtained glowing letters from three of his colleagues, testifying to his consultative management style and creative leadership.

The best evidence is to be found not in what a candidate's friends say but in the judgments attested to by a variety of individuals who hold responsible positions at the candidate's campus. What does the chair of the senate say about the candidate's commitment to upholding the appropriate authority of the faculty? What does the chair of the curriculum committee report about the candidate's attitude toward rethinking requirements? What does the chair of the appointments committee tell about the candidate's standards for appointments, promotions, and tenure? What do department chairs relate about the candidate's approach to making budgetary decisions? Do the chairs find the candidate accessible, resourceful, fair-minded, and committed to enhancing academic quality? Do other administrators or administrative assistants view the candidate as thoughtful or impulsive, patient or irritable, collegial or overbearing, forgiving or vindictive?

During an interview of a few hours, the candidate may maintain a false front to members of a search committee. But those who have long observed the candidate's character, including at times of personal confrontation or moments of institutional crisis, are beyond being fooled.

Thus, when the list of finalists is determined, each should be informed that at least one or, better yet, several members of the committee will be speaking to or, preferably, visiting with key members of the academic community at the candidate's school. And while a candidate may request that a particular person not be contacted if that individual is thought to be negatively biased, a candidate who objects to the whole procedure should be passed over. For however strong the candidate's desire to retain confidentiality, it is outweighed by the committee's obligation to make the soundest possible decision.

If the information thus obtained suggests that the administrator's performance was less than first-rate, the committee may reasonably assume the person will do no better at the next position. The administrator who micromanaged one campus is a good bet to try to do so at the next. The administrator who wasted money at one institution is unlikely to spend it wisely at another. During interviews, a candidate may give the impression of welcoming constructive criticism, but if numerous colleagues who have worked with the person report to the contrary, their testimony should be considered decisive.

Indeed, were I required to select an administrator by relying either on a vita, letters of recommendation, and interviews, or solely on the judgments of numerous previous colleagues, I would choose the latter. But search committees do not face this forced option. They can continue to consider the usual information while supplementing it with the best available evidence. Such a procedure would lead to greater satisfaction with the performance of those we entrust with administrative responsibilities. And achieving that goal is the measure of success for every search committee.

SOURCES

Unless otherwise noted, all materials are copyrighted by Steven M. Cahn and can be used only with his permission.

1. *A New Introduction to Philosophy*, Harper & Row, 1971.

2. *Philosophy and Phenomenological Research*, XXVII, 4, 1977. Used by permission of the journal.

3. *Questions about God*, eds. Steven M. Cahn and David Shatz, Oxford University Press, 2002.

4. *A New Introduction to Philosophy*, Harper & Row, 1971.

5. *Analysis*, 37, 2, 1977.

6. *Philosophy for the 21st Century: A Comprehensive Reader*, Oxford University Press, 2003.

7. *The Reconstructionist*, XXXI, 16, 1965. Used by permission of the journal.

8. *Newsletter on Teaching Philosophy*, November, 1988. Used by permission of the journal.

9. *Philosophy and Faith*, ed. David Shatz, McGraw-Hill, 2002.

10. *A New Introduction to Philosophy*, Harper & Row, 1971.

11. *A New Introduction to Philosophy*, Harper & Row, 1971.

12. *Academe*, 83, 1, 1997.

13. *Journal of Social Philosophy*, 28, 1, 1997. Used by permission of the journal.

14. *The Chronicle of Higher Education*, XXXV, 30, 1989. Used by permission of the journal.

15. *Analysis* 47, 3, 1987; 49, 3, 1989; 51, 2, 1991.

16. Section I is from *The Journal of Aesthetics and Art Criticism*, XXXIV, 1, 1975. Used by permission of The American Society for Aesthetics. L. Michael Griffel is professor of music at Hunter College and the Graduate Center of the City University of New York. Section II is from *Philosophical Explorations: Freedom, God, and Goodness*. Prometheus Books, 1989.

17. *The Shakespeare Newsletter*, XXXVIII, 3-4, 1989. Used by permission of the journal.

18. *John Dewey: The Later Works*, vol. 13, ed. Jo Ann Boydston, Southern Illinois University Press, 1988.

19. *AAUP Bulletin*, 59, 3, 1973.

20. *Teaching Philosophy*, 4, 1, 1981. Used by permission of the journal.

21. *Newsletter on Teaching Philosophy*, Fall, 1986. Used by permission of the American Philosophical Association.

22. *Newsletter on Teaching Philosophy*, June, 1988. Used by permission of the American Philosophical Association.

23. *AAHE Bulletin*, 50, 2, 1997. Used by permission of the American Association of Higher Education.

BIBLIOGRAPHY OF
STEVEN M. CAHN

BOOKS AUTHORED

Fate, Logic, and Time
Yale University Press, 1967
Reprinted by Ridgeview Publishing Company, 1982

A New Introduction to Philosophy
Harper & Row, 1971
Reprinted by University Press of America, 1986

The Eclipse of Excellence: A Critique of American Higher Education
(Foreword by Charles Frankel)
Public Affairs Press, 1973

Education and the Democratic Ideal
Nelson-Hall Company, 1979

Saints and Scamps: Ethics in Academia
Rowman & Littlefield, 1986
Revised Edition, 1994

Philosophical Explorations: Freedom, God, and Goodness
Prometheus Books, 1989

Puzzles & Perplexities: Collected Essays
Rowman & Littlefield, 2002

BOOKS EDITED

Philosophy of Art and Aesthetics: From Plato to Wittgenstein
(with Frank A. Tillman)
Harper & Row, 1969

The Philosophical Foundations of Education
Harper & Row, 1970

Philosophy of Religion
Harper & Row, 1970

Classics of Western Philosophy
Hackett Publishing Company, 1977
Second Edition, 1985
Third Edition, 1990
Fourth Edition, 1995
Fifth Edition, 1999
Sixth Edition, 2003

New Studies in the Philosophy of John Dewey
University Press of New England, 1977

Scholars Who Teach: The Art of College Teaching
Nelson–Hall Company, 1978

Contemporary Philosophy of Religion
(with David Shatz)
Oxford University Press, 1982

Reason at Work: Introductory Readings in Philosophy
(with Patricia Kitcher and George Sher)
Harcourt Brace Jovanovich, 1984
Second Edition, 1990
Third Edition (also with Peter J. Markie), 1995

Morality, Responsibility, and the University: Studies in Academic Ethics
Temple University Press, 1990

Affirmative Action and the University: A Philosophical Inquiry
Temple University Press, 1993

Twentieth-Century Ethical Theory
(with Joram G. Haber)
Prentice Hall, 1995

The Affirmative Action Debate
Routledge, 1995.
Second Edition, 2002

Classics of Modern Political Theory: Machiavelli to Mill
Oxford University Press, 1996

Classic and Contemporary Readings in the Philosophy of Education
McGraw–Hill, 1997

Ethics: History, Theory, and Contemporary Issues
(with Peter Markie)
Oxford University Press, 1998
Second Edition, 2002

Exploring Philosophy: An Introductory Anthology
Oxford University Press, 2000

Classics of Political and Moral Philosophy
Oxford University Press, 2002

Questions About God
(with David Shatz)
Oxford University Press, 2002

Morality and Public Policy
(with Tziporah Kasachkoff)
Prentice Hall, 2003

Knowledge and Reality
(with Maureen Eckert and Robert Buckley)
Prentice Hall, 2003

Philosophy for the 21st Century: A Comprehensive Reader
Oxford University Press, 2003

ABOUT THE AUTHOR

Steven M. Cahn is Professor of Philosophy at the Graduate Center of The City University of New York, where he served as Provost and Vice President for Academic Affairs and then Acting President. He received his A.B. from Columbia College and his Ph.D. from Columbia University. He has previously taught at Dartmouth College, Vassar College, the University of Rochester, New York University, and at the University of Vermont, where he headed the Department of Philosophy.

He served as a program officer at the Exxon Education Foundation, as acting director for humanities at the Rockefeller Foundation, and as director of the Division of General Programs at the National Endowment for the Humanities. He chaired the American Philosophical Association's Committee on the Teaching of Philosophy and is currently President of the John Dewey Foundation.

In addition to the numerous books he has authored or edited, he serves as general editor of four ongoing series: *Blackwell Philosophy Guides, Blackwell Readings in Philosophy, Issues in Academic Ethics,* and *Critical Essays on the Classics* (the latter two published by Rowman & Littlefield).